Religious Studies Beyond the Discipline

NAASR Working Papers

Series Editor: Emily D. Crews, University of Chicago Divinity School

NAASR Working Papers provides a venue for publishing the latest research carried out by scholars who understand religion to be an historical element of human cognition, practice, and organization. Whether monographs or multi-authored collections, the volumes published in this series all reflect timely, cutting edge work that takes seriously both the need for developing bold theories as well as rigorous testing and debate concerning the scope of our tools and the implications of our studies. *NAASR Working Papers* therefore assess the current state-of-the-art while charting new ways forward in the academic study of religion.

Founding Series Editor: Brad Stoddard, McDaniel College in Westminster, Maryland

Religious Studies Beyond the Discipline

On the Future of a Humanities Ph.D.

Edited by
Russell T. McCutcheon

eQuinox

SHEFFIELD UK   BRISTOL CT

Published by Equinox Publishing Ltd.

U.K.: Office 415, The Workstation, 15 Paternoster Row, Sheffield, South Yorkshire S1 2BX

U.S.A.: ISD, 70 Enterprise Drive, Bristol, CT 06010

www.equinoxpub.com

First published 2024

ISBN-13   978 1 80050 543 8   (hardback)
          978 1 80050 544 5   (paperback)
          978 1 80050 545 2   (ePDF)
          978 1 80050 616 9   (ePub)

British Library Cataloguing-in-Publication Data

A catalogue record for this book is available from the British Library.

Library of Congress Cataloging-in-Publication Data

Names: McCutcheon, Russell T., 1961- editor.
Title: Religious studies beyond the discipline : on the future of a humanities Ph.D. / edited by Russell T. McCutcheon.
Description: Sheffield, South Yorkshire ; Bristol, CT : Equinox Publishing Ltd, 2024. | Series: NAASR working papers | Includes bibliographical references and index. |
Summary: "The aim for the volume is to initiate and then move forward a conversation among future, current, and recent graduate students as well as those who train them concerning the content, process, and purpose of acquiring advanced research skills in the early twenty-first century university"—Provided by publisher.
Identifiers: LCCN 2024018261 (print) | LCCN 2024018262 (ebook) | ISBN 9781800505438 (hardback) | ISBN 9781800505445 (paperback) | ISBN 9781800505452 (ePDF) | ISBN 9781800506169 (ePub)
Subjects: LCSH: Religion—Study and teaching (Higher)
Classification: LCC BL41 .R436 2024 (print) | LCC BL41 (ebook) | DDC 200.71/1—dc23/eng/20240521
LC record available at https://lccn.loc.gov/2024018261
LC ebook record available at https://lccn.loc.gov/2024018262

Typeset by JS Typesetting Ltd, Porthcawl, Mid Glamorgan

This book is dedicated to all those willing to entertain that things could be otherwise

... graduate school in the arts and sciences prepares students for jobs that don't exist. And while it prepares them, it teaches them to want those jobs above all others.

—Leonard Cassuto & Robert Weisbuch, *The New Ph.D.* (2021)

Contents

Acknowledgements

To open this volume, I need to acknowledge not only some of my colleagues here in the Department of Religious Studies at the University of Alabama, who have consistently been attentive to an assortment of professional and institutional issues that, to their own detriment, others across our field have yet to take all that seriously. I'd also like to single out the students with whom we've worked—especially the M.A. students who, despite many having dreams of an academic career, have often reconsidered their future in light of the plain realities of higher education today; they've often engaged in the sometimes-tough work of reinventing themselves (always with our program's assistance, I'd like to think) and that needs to be recognized. Their successes upon graduation, in a host of careers, also deserve to be celebrated.

I must also extend my thanks to those in leadership positions in a small number of doctoral programs around the U.S. who were bold enough to accept my invitation to join a volume that, perhaps in the eyes of some, may be just a little controversial. As readers may have anticipated, quite a few invitations were extended when I first conceived this project, all going to those who are involved in leading some of the U.S.'s doctoral programs in the study of religion—people who, though not having a free reign, of course, are in the position to help move our programs to a position of delivering more for the students who are enrolled in them and the profession that relies upon them; for a variety of reasons these invitations were mostly declined, however. That the gravity of the situation and the implications for our entire field of a humanities doctoral job market collapsing in on itself—a problem decades in the making, as will be discussed later—were enough to inspire those respondents who accepted the invitation (to whatever extent they agree with the volume's proposals) is something for which I am also grateful.

My thanks as well goes to the many others contributing to this book, from the two former Alabama grad students—Erica Bennett and Jacob Barrett—who, in the summer of 2022, hosted and produced a podcast series (the edited transcriptions for which appear in the opening to this volume), to those who agreed to be interviewed for that series and talk about their experiences in graduate schools (as students or as faculty) and on the job market. I must also mention my four co-authors—Andrew Ali Aghapour, Shannon Trosper Schorey, Thomas Whitley, and Vaia Touna—who, despite participating in a poorly attended remote session on these topics (held as part of our southeast region's annual scholarly meeting a couple year ago), nonetheless all agreed to dive back in and develop a co-written piece on the need to revise how we approach the Ph.D. in our field and then try to get it published. I also wish to thank another of my colleagues, Richard

Newton, who, as editor of Equinox's *The Bulletin for the Study of Religion*, previously published our co-written manifesto (as well as reading and then commenting on the entire book's manuscript before it went to the press), as well as acknowledge once again Janet Joyce, Director of Equinox Publishing, who agreed to publish a volume anchored by it (appearing in a series that Emily Crews edits for the North American Association for the Study of Religion [NAASR]). That Janet and her whole team (with this book involving Val Hall, Sarah Lee, Hamish Ironside, and Mark Lee) have long played a foundational role in pressing the edges of our field in new and sometimes challenging directions—whether via her own press, Equinox, or the other academic publishers for which she had previously worked and where some of my own publications once appeared—needs to be said (and, yes, celebrated) publicly far more than it is. And my thanks once again go to Andie Alexander for agreeing to make the book's index.

   I must also credit Josh Patterson (former Research Director for Higher Education Studies at the research firm SoundRocket) and Robert Townsend (Program Director for Humanities, Arts, and Culture within the American Academy of Arts and Sciences) for both assisting me with navigating some of the sources for Appendix 1 and 2, for providing feedback on an earlier draft of those two short pieces. I should also mention Matt Sheedy, who provided feedback of his own on the appendices, along with acknowledging: Christopher Hooker (Director of Membership and Programs for the Society of Biblical Literature)—who provided context concerning recent gaps in job openings reporting; Scott Sederstrom (a member of the Department of Research and Public Policy with the American Association of University Professors [AAUP]); and Kelly H. Kang (Project Officer for the Survey of Earned Doctorates, sponsored by the National Center for Science and Engineering Statistics [NCSES] and the National Science Foundation [NSF]), the latter two offering helpful advice on additional sources of national data. And, finally, my wife, Marcia Hay-McCutcheon, herself an audiologist and faculty member in UA's Department of Communicative Disorders, kindly helped out this humanities professor by working with the data that I had assembled to make the graph that appears in Appendix 2 using SigmaPlot.

   Before closing, I should mention all those over the recent decades who have trained in the study of religion, let alone any number of adjacent fields in the humanities, and who, sooner or later, found themselves needing to make the tough decision to reinvent themselves in order not just to pay their bills but also to pursue their hopes and their interests. I was lucky enough to land a tenure-track position in southwest Missouri back in 1996, but only after my wife and I began making our initial preparations to head back to Canada as my three years as a full-time instructor at the University of Tennessee was coming to an end; during those three years I had mailed out my share of unsuccessful applications to universities in the U.S. and Canada—not to mention a proposal for a postdoc submitted to a university in Australia for a project on the study of religion in Indonesia (as but one among many former colonial sites where the field took root). While I would be insincere of me to think that such early frustrations conformed to what so many others have gone through while making careers for themselves outside academia, I at least wish to record here that this volume is based in part on an awareness of at least some of their hard-won experience and the challenges that they faced. As for those to whom the volume is dedicated, i.e., those currently exerting influence on graduate programs as well as those now immersed in their classes, writing dissertations, or even those aspiring to enroll someday, I close by saying that I hope there's something of value for you in the following pages—something that, for faculty, enables you to inspire some practical (even fundamental) revisions to your graduate programs' requirements and processes or, now speaking directly to the students, something that allows you to make some strategic choices of your own within a profession and an institution that can, at times, be surprisingly conservative.

Foreword

Raj Balkaran

I completed my doctorate in 2015, and with it my training on how to land an academic job. My C.V. was stacked—presentations, publications, administration, teaching, awards, grants, you name it—and, as such, I was confident that, given my skills and experience, I would land an academic job, despite the abysmal odds. I was short-listed for three positions during my first year on the academic job market, but in each case the job went to the individual whose research interest was most aligned with the posting. I soon learned that it wasn't a question of my ability to land a job—on the contrary, people tend to want to put me to work wherever I go, paid or otherwise!—rather, it was an issue of *there being no job to land*. My expertise is in Sanskrit narrative texts (ancient Indian mythological stories essentially), and I haven't come across an academic job seeking such expertise since I defended my dissertation.

Shortly after completing the doctorate, I turned to entrepreneurship out of dire necessity, at first kicking and screaming. Now, some eight years later, I've managed to generate a would-be professorial salary drawing from my expertise. Some are lucky enough to have a job, more fortunate still are those who land a career. The most fortunate folks, in my view, are those who have a calling, a mission, and find a way to monetize that mission. In my case that mission entails the production and dissemination of knowledge on Sanskrit narrative literature, particularly for the sake of public education. While scholarly production is a labor of love, my teaching is monetized. I used to refer to myself as the world's most successful unemployed scholar; I now refer to myself as the world's most successful self-employed scholar.

My bills are paid through meaningful and impactful work managing an online school which I founded, operating a flourishing one-on-one consultancy practice, delivering talks, and running international in-person retreats. But this work doesn't thwart my scholarly calling: it empowers it. Since completing the doctorate, I've produced two scholarly monographs, a public book consisting of translations, a landmark co-edited volume, two co-edited conference proceedings, twelve journal articles, and six book chapters. I also regularly present at premier venues in my field, hold multiple service positions and collaborate with colleagues. The fundamental distinction between my own path and that of my successful professorial colleagues is that I've had to find a way to earn my keep beyond the academy. I never imagined this sort of scholarly success could be the case for a scholar situated beyond the academy proper, yet this path may well serve as a model for others.

I accept semester-long university sessional teaching contracts where I can (eight to date) because I love teaching undergrads. But I do so from a position of self-sufficiency, not needing to succumb to the exploitative adjunct rat race. I need not panic if the contract isn't renewed, nor worry about how to pay my bills on an income below the poverty line. I would wholeheartedly welcome a professorship proper, were it the right fit. However, I have found a way not only to survive beyond the professoriate, but to thrive as a productive, connected, respected scholar and public intellectual. Beyond teaching continuing studies at my own online school and at premier online platforms, such as the Oxford Centre for Hindu Studies, I host a popular podcast on the New Books Network (now consisting of over 300 episodes) where I interview authors on their new books in the broad field of Indian religions. This enterprise, much as my continuing studies teaching, goes a long way towards bridging the public/academy divide.

I found a way to monetize my skills and interests, but only through a very painful and difficult trial by fire. A great many of the skills required for this process could have been imparted during my doctoral training. More invaluable would have been the permission, and validation, of seeking meaningful work beyond the professoriate. This prospect is what I now strive to convey to any humanities Ph.D. who will listen. Beyond scores of informal conversations, I've been invited to formally share my "alt-ac" experiences on three occasions: at the University of Calgary's Department of Classics and Religion in 2020 (my doctoral alma mater), at the annual conference on South Asia at the University of Wisconsin–Madison in 2022, and most recently, in 2023, at the University of Toronto's Department for the Study of Religion (my alma mater for both my B.A. and M.A.). In each case I shared paths forward whereby one could monetize one's doctoral expertise (through teaching, consultancy or content creation) and work for oneself, all the while continuing to engage in impactful scholarly work beyond the professoriate. I vividly recall a question in my Calgary talk (at a department which, by the way, was religious studies when I began my degree in 2011 and had to merge to become classics and religion by the time I finished four years later, for the sake of its survival) about how faculty might be able to support graduate students toward such an alternative path. I responded that it would be unrealistic—and perhaps even unfair—to expect an individual who has known only the traditional academic path their whole working life to guide someone beyond that path. But now, just a few years later, I've changed my tune: it is our collective responsibility as a discipline to navigate the challenges and transformations afoot. To my surprise, a number of traditional "old school" professors have approached me looking for insight on how to guide their brilliant students for whom academic jobs simply do not exist. But not nearly enough of our colleagues are thinking along these lines, hence the need for the publication at hand.

Poignantly provocative, *Religious Studies Beyond the Discipline* is therefore nothing if not timely. The winds of change are well upon us, and we all know what happens to branches that do not bend. Business as usual is not an option, rather it's a sure-fire way of shooting ourselves in the foot as a field. The many insightful and creative strategies outlined herein need not be adopted wholesale, but the impetus behind them needs to be heeded: we are in the midst of a systemic, existential crisis. The ivory tower is on fire, folks. I deeply value my traditional doctoral training, and continue to leverage it for my current research and teaching, even as a public intellectual. So, rather than a "Ph.D. 2.0," perhaps a "Ph.D. Plus" would have been in order so as to offer a vision of, and tools towards, thriving beyond the professoriate. A colossal amount of blood, sweat and tears would have been saved with very simple instructional additions to my doctoral program. This path was truly arduous at the outset, but now it's beyond fulfilling. Luckily, I was able to find a way to continue scholarly production, but other doctoral graduates have not been so fortunate. What needs to change for us to set religion Ph.D.'s up for success? You may disagree about how to answer this question, but we can no longer ignore the necessity of posing it. This landmark publication needs to be read—and read widely. *Religious Studies Beyond the Discipline* is more than a manifesto: it sparks a conversation, a crucial conversation, that we'd be wise to collectively engage, advance, enrich and action. Our very survival as a discipline depends upon it.

Toronto, November 2023

Raj Balkaran is a prolific self-employed scholar of Sanskrit narrative literature who earned his Ph.D. at the University of Calgary in 2015. Among his publications are *The Goddess and the King in Indian Myth* (Routledge, 2020) and the co-edited book, *Visions and Revisions in Sanskrit Narrative* (Australian National University Press, 2024). He teaches at the Oxford Centre for Hindu Studies and, since 2018, has hosted over 300 episodes of the New Books in Indian Religions podcast.

Preface

As I finalize this volume, I am just a few weeks out from hosting a webinar for the American Academy of Religion's Academic Relations Committee (ARC), which I currently chair, that was devoted to the topic of department mergers (a topic well known to many in our field). The guest was my onetime colleague (when, in the late 1990s, I worked at what was once known as Southwest Missouri State University, but now Missouri State), Steve Berkwitz. Although the head of their prior Department of Religious Studies, he became, just in the summer of 2023, the first head of the newly formed (and considerably larger) unit, the Department of Languages, Cultures, and Religions, which combined what many campuses would call their Department of Modern Languages with Religious Studies. This merger, he told the twenty-five or so who signed on to the webinar, was part of a campus-wide exercise that had been developing for a couple years, resulting in many departments moving and/or merging, something that affected even entire colleges (e.g., The College of Public Affairs, of which religious studies had long been a member, was rolled into the College of Humanities and Social Sciences). Understanding this reorganization as therefore not specifically directed at the humanities, he made evident that he thought, at least at Missouri State, it could be viewed as a real opportunity for the department (i.e., there's power in numbers, as they say), what with the ever present possibility of attrition among faculty lines (such as when retirements go unfilled due to any number of administrative reasons, among which would be budgetary shortfalls and the long predicted "demographic cliff" getting closer, when the anticipated decline in the number of U.S. high school graduates will surely lead to any number of ramifications for university campuses—such as an increased competition among them for students). That some in the Q&A were not as optimistic about mergers, seeing them instead as the advance guard for eventual downsizing (sometimes known as retrenchments by the rhetorically minded on a campus), deserves to be noted. As the planning for that webinar was under way, it was impossible to ignore the national news concerning the ongoing cuts and protests (among faculty, staff, *and* students) taking place at West Virginia University—that state's so-called flagship public land-grant university. Due to whatever extent to a reported $45 million deficit, the administration had already announced what many saw as a radical restructuring of campus (or what the administration calls a transformation), entailing the loss of many majors, departments (e.g., possibly World Languages, Literatures, and Linguistics as well as Public Administration), and faculty lines, resulting in faculty resigning and departing, retiring early, or receiving so-called RIF notices (reduction in force—a convenient euphemism for being fired); as of early October 2023 it was announced there that, due to the many early retirements, *only* 70 or so faculty would be fired, instead of the original announcement of up to 143. In contact with Aaron Gale, the former head of WVU's prior Department of Religious Studies, it quickly became apparent that their major had already been lost in 2021, that in 2022 they had been re-merged with philosophy (after having been an autonomous unit since 2004), and that today the department is made up of only three full-time faculty (two of whom are teaching professors) and a variety of part-time lecturers (who all received their RIF notices). Also happening as that mergers webinar was being planned was the announcement that, due to low student numbers, Miami University of Ohio would likely be cutting up to eighteen majors. As the local news reported it: "Students at Miami University may no longer be able to major in some humanities programs, such as American studies, religion or health communication ..." Contacting a colleague there, James Hanges (the religious studies chair), it was apparent that their department was already strategizing on how to weather such cuts as best they could, to ensure both subject areas for students and jobs for faculty and staff were retained as much as possible. (Representatives of WVU's and Miami of Ohio's departments were guests on the very next webinar I hosted, by the way, providing an opportunity for colleagues to be updated on what was happening on their campuses.) And on my own campus, despite a variety of very real successes in our department over the past two decades—after being poised to lose the major and possibly close, back in 2000—a long process across campus of developing of a revised undergraduate Core Curriculum (something happening at colleges all across the U.S. over the past decade or so) resulted in a new set of General Education requirements that, predictably, cut the overall numbers of credit hours required of an undergraduate student—a cut largely coming at the expense of the sorts of Core classes that a typical humanities program such as our own would routinely offer. After all, we're a unit that, despite having a strong undergraduate major and what I like to think of as a rather innovative, skills-based M.A. program, still offers well over 90% of our annual credit hour production as so-called service courses to other majors, all of whom are aiming to satisfy their Core requirements. New Core requirements that result in more units competing for access to students who are satisfying fewer credit hours understandably sends a shiver up the backs of those faculty members who are paying attention—even in seemingly successful or secure departments.

If you add to all this the Zoom session that I had earlier in the Fall of 2023 with the faculty in a small private liberal arts school in the Carolinas, concerned for their own unit's future well-being and wanting to bounce ideas off of someone from another campus, let alone the University of Vermont's need to restructure their religious studies department back in 2021, in order to save it (which they successfully did), after it was named as one of the twenty-seven programs within UVM's College of Arts & Sciences that might close, not to mention colleagues at two different small liberal arts colleges (SLACs each with less than 70 total faculty members) where, in one case, a high of seven or eight faculty lines in the study of religion (decades ago) has now been reduced to 0.5 lines and, in the other, the loss of several majors on their campus is resulting in a combined cross-disciplinary humanities major (possibly pitched at business students by being sold as focused on leadership), and you arrive at what I see as sufficient anecdotal reporting that should make even a skeptical faculty member rather concerned for the future of the humanities in general and undergraduate programs in religious studies in particular. I won't even add to this list the Chair at yet another SLAC who just messaged me the other day to chat about troubling signals that they're now receiving from the administration concerning their unit's future, let alone the colleague at another midwestern SLAC who just presented a paper at a national conference on the very real challenges to her small unit or the just posted news on social media that Bradley University's joint Philosophy and Religions Studies Department, along with its majors and minors, is, according to their campus's president, now on the chopping block. Nor will I mention in any real detail the colleague at Wheaton, yet another SLAC, who alerted me just the other day of a process of department mergers now happening there, followed by potential "sunsetting" of a variety of majors—despite a better-than-expected number of incoming first year students this academic year. (Last year's budget cuts at Wheaton resulted in their administration rolling out a plan to decrease the number of full-time faculty by 13% by the year 2025.) And neither will I add any detail about the various college-level mergers that just happened at Virginia Commonwealth University (which also involved history, philosophy, and religious studies being combined) nor what I just learned from another midwestern private university where, although the news does not yet seem to be public, all of these same issues are suddenly of grave concern across campus—not to mention who knows how many other programs that, by the time this book is published, will have joined all of these as autonomous units no more, or as programs with no majors, thereby reduced to a mere service role on their campuses. Topping this all off with the realization that *none of this is coming from out of the blue* but, instead, that, in addition to the very recent impact of COVID budget cuts on campuses, *trends in higher education have steadily been going in this obvious direction for decades*, makes one wonder where the doctoral programs in our field think that their graduates—almost all of whom are still being trained in narrow specialties *as if* they will one day become tenure-track faculty members—are going to find employment. For even if units are not closed outright, the strategy of shrinking the humanities faculty in general, and in our field in particular, through slow and steady attrition (by not replacing lines vacated by retirements), surely needs to catch the eye of doctoral programs in our field.

And so, with all of this in mind, you can only imagine how I read the recruiting materials from one of the main U.S. doctoral programs in our field that only the other day came across my desk, which, along with a flyer for bulletin boards, contained a letter to colleagues that concluded with the line: "We have very good placement records, with many of our graduates getting jobs at top-tiered research universities." Despite recognizing it as a marketing slogan, even a meagre sense of responsibility to the doctoral students whom we train means that much of this claim needs scrutiny—What counts as "very good"? What is the historic trend for your placement rate? Which jobs in particular have your alums landed on these "top-tiered" campuses? The devil's in the details, as they say; but such unpacking, let alone retooling their programs to help their current and future graduate students to meet the needs of the moment, is often not all that appealing to doctoral programs intent on delivering "the same old same old."

Which brings me to one final, prefatory anecdote, more directly in step with the theme of this volume. In the spring of 2015 I visited one of the field's main doctoral schools to give a talk on teaching the introductory class, During my visit I heard from a couple sources—both graduate students repeating what they had been told as well as directly from a faculty member—that the primary purpose for students to be enrolled in a doctoral program (or, perhaps, at that particular one) was "to write a field-changing dissertation." Sure, being professionalized as a grad student, such as gaining publications of your own, acquiring teaching experience, serving on committees and helping to organize events, etc., can be of value to a developing career but, or so this brand of advice was conveyed to me, that is all a distraction from your primary purpose: to write a field-changing dissertation.

I admit that I found this rationale and career advice, coming at what may now seem to be a long time ago, rather odd, even risky. Without aiming to undermine too seriously their own supervisors, I made sure that those students knew my thoughts on such counsel; and, at dinner one evening with a faculty member and yet other students, I pushed back in the following way, doing so in that collegial give-and-take manner that we all know so well when a controversial topic comes up at a conference or in a meeting.

First off, given what I'll just go ahead and qualify as the atrocious labor conditions of the humanities (conditions that were already pretty poor in 2015, despite the more recent COVID-19 pandemic making us now think that this was longer ago than it actually was) the imprimatur of the school where one trains, the reputation of one's doctoral supervisor, as well as the topic of one's dissertation may end up mattering far less than the practical skills that a candidate brings to the table on day one of their first job—a job that, judging by the national statistics, is very likely to be well outside academia. Sure, some might land a job interview at an elite school, with a light teaching load, small class sizes, and a large department filled with other specialists in your area—thereby affording them the luxury of focusing all of their writing and classes on, say, just Krishna's first speech in the Gita. But then again, they may be lucky just to get an interview at a dramatically different sort of department, a small one (a joint philosophy/religious studies program with only two or three faculty, perhaps) in which they'll teach three or four (or more?) different classes each semester, across a broad range of more or less general topics in the field that have little to do with the content of their specialized doctoral work. As important as their research may be to such applicants, the ability of their new colleagues to have confidence that they'll know what they're doing when the first day of classes rolls around could, conceivably, outweigh many of those other things that such candidates have been taught by their supervisors to value on their C.V. And adding to that a recognition that even more of those doctoral graduates will never have campus interviews and, instead, will be reinventing themselves for lives and careers well outside of academia, where they will be challenged, just to gain entry to such positions, to identify the far broader skills that they acquired doing all those close readings and all that fieldwork, well, you can imagine how I heard that exceedingly privileged and (at least to my ears) out-of-touch advice that these students were being given. And, yes, the students all knew this as well, since they were not naïve to the labor conditions of academia let alone the teaching skills, to name but one example, being gained by their peers enrolled at other institutions.

To dig a little deeper into what for the time being I'll just call curious advice, I'm not even sure what counts as "a field-changing dissertation"; for even if such a unicorn exists (and I'm doubtful it does) then it's certainly not changing the field as a dissertation but, instead, as the book that it (might) eventually become; not growing on trees, anyone who has written one can tell you that books sometimes take years to write (aka making revisions to your dissertation, at least for many people's first academic book today), let alone the length of time required to be submitted to the press, gain an acquisition editor's attention, and then be refereed, revised, resubmitted, contracted, copyedited, proofed, proofed again, indexed, and, one day, published. And we've not yet factored in how long it then takes to get into people's hands, to get into libraries, to attract a readership, to be reviewed—if it is even reviewed, that is—and, if indeed "field changing," the time that it'll likely take for that book to weather the initial criticisms and somehow rise above them. All this is no easy task, what with happenstance playing as much, or probably more, of a role as does the supposed merit of the argument. Then, it needs to get into classrooms and on the syllabi of graduate seminars, be cited in the articles and books of yet other scholars, and then onto comprehensive exam reading lists ...; after all, despite a campus's reputation for some as liberal enclaves, academic fields are conservative beasts and their members generally do not willingly change what they do (the very fact of this book and the diversity of views evident in its pages makes that evident). Judging by my own career, in which I happen to have had a first book that gained the attention of some in the field, I can report that, when an alternative is proposed, there's usually a lot of kicking and screaming on the part of those who have done it this and only this way for their entire careers. As did their supervisors. And theirs. For there's an awful lot invested in doing things a certain way—not to mention sheer social inertia. Change doesn't come naturally to any group, academia included. And so, despite the tremendous feeling of accomplishment that justifiably comes from finishing and successfully defending your dissertation, changing a field (if it ever actually happens, apart from those so-called Kuhnian paradigm shifts we see once in a very long time) is a many-decades-long, incremental process that involves far more people than the mythical lone writer penning a compelling argument or a revolutionary treatise. The question that all of those game-changers must ask of themselves, then, is what they will each be doing in the decades that it takes for this to happen—if it happens. Hopefully paying the bills by means of those skills that they acquired throughout their graduate schooling, no? (Notice that I'm not even going down the road of finding that work, whatever it is, to be challenging and rewarding, let alone lucrative—for today, such goals are a bridge too far for many of those who worked so hard to earn a Ph.D. but who, with little to no assistance from their graduate programs, have been forced to look to industry, or government, or NGOs, etc., for work.)

So, despite this episode taking place several years before the current problems which were outlined in the opening had taken full effect, my counter-advice to those students (and anyone else who, since then, has asked) was to be ambitious and aim high, sure; but also to recognize that, like any institution, there are a variety of factors at work in determining their long term success in academia, many of which are well beyond any individual's control (i.e., everything from the content of those confidential letters of reference that attend job applications to the strength of the economy and the always changeable national or even local political winds—let alone the shifting priorities of a campus, where plenty of money may sometimes exist but not for strengthening humanities education). So, while aiming to write a field-changing dissertation sounds like a great idea, it also sounds like an awfully long range goal that, to a student's detriment, overlooks the many short term accomplishments (from "do you have teaching experience?" to "what broader skills did you gain and how can they be put to work both insider but, importantly, also outside the university?") that will more than likely determine whether they're around to accept all of the accolades that their first book (might) earn for them some day. Simply put, we must not overlook that it's not unusual for each year's Nobel Prize in this or that discipline to be awarded for (sometimes unheralded) work carried out decades before.

I've thought of that campus visit often over the past several years, always cognizant of how much worse the situation keeps getting (as the other anecdotes should make clear). While it is heartening to know that, since then, that program has developed a series of professionalizing workshops, offering regular sessions for their grad students, from what I hear it is still all geared toward landing and excelling at a campus interview and thus a tenure-track position—outcomes of doctoral training in the humanities that, today, are very rare accomplishments. To our field's detriment, empowering graduate students through novel program requirements and assignments to excel in almost any career is still well beyond most of our departments.

What should be evident, then, is that the topics addressed in this volume have been on my mind for some time; the problems in academia that it recounts and tries to address are far older than that, of course. In fact, along with focusing on the professionalizing needed to try to succeed in academia (e.g., a piece that I wrote entitled "Theses on Professionalization," first published back in 2007, along with replies to it from early career scholars that appeared in 2018, taking into account the changing conditions of the profession) I've also been writing on issues in the job market pretty much my whole career; case in point, my first pieces on this latter topics were published in 1997 and 1998; although I was hardly the first in our field to see these challenges as concerning, I admit that I find far too few of our colleagues to be publishing on, or even talking publicly and proactively about, the situation in higher ed. Perhaps my focus is linked to when I was a grad student, in Toronto, and what I happened to be studying. For graduate school from the mid-1980s to the early 1990s was a time when the inevitable retirements of those who had been hired to teach the waves of baby boomers first entering college in the mid-1960s meant (or so we were reassured at the time) that there would be jobs galore for us (those retiring faculty were, in many cases, just a bit older than the baby boomers themselves); as it turned out, this was not to be the case. What did result, however, was a sobering lesson in not putting too much stock in projections, at least when it came to the academic job market. And so, as someone who, as a doctoral student, didn't even specialize in a tradition (i.e., didn't get his hands dirty, as I was often told then and now), the logic—if that's even the right word for an apparent meritocracy that is often anything but—of the academic job market was evident to me very early on (as was the need to persuade more in the field that this was a problem). Those anticipated jobs never materialized because of the (at least at the time) unforeseen funding cuts followed by colleges deciding not to fill many of the vacancies created by those retirements (those, at least, did happen). And thus the turn on campuses across North America to a far greater reliance on limited term contract, sessional, part-time, or in a word, contingent labor.

In fact, it was in direct relation to those early experiences as well as my career's start as a one year full-time instructor (for a total of three years at the University of Tennessee), all of which were reinforced by how my current colleagues also viewed these issues, that the recent M.A. degree that our department (inaugurated back in 2017—something that we began discussing as early as 2013 but which we began planning in earnest in 2015) was explicitly organized around the assumption that the world more than likely did not need another graduate program in the academic study of religion, despite how differently we saw ourselves to practice it. But taking seriously how we understood our contributions (i.e., an explicit use of social theory to study religion as but an element of ordinary and historical cultural practices), we soon settled on a way to stay true to how we thought the field ought to work while also aiming to equip our future students with what many have long called practical, transferable skills—those that, or so we hoped, would do these students well in a variety of futures. For all along we were not naïve to the likelihood that few of our graduate students would wish to pursue doctoral studies and even those who applied and were lucky enough to be accepted into such programs would face an uncertain future once they'd successfully defended their dissertations. So digital skills—whether thick (by which I mean using computers to create or analyze our data) or more in the vein of the public humanities variety (by which we communicate our findings to increasingly wide audiences)—became a major focus of our graduate program from the outset. And, so far at least, it has proved to be a wise investment, and one that has had increasing impact on our undergraduate program as well, not to mention some colleagues' own research and grant-writing.

My hope, then, is that enough people in our field have by now tired of the terribly disconnected "field-changing dissertation" rationale for why we continue to train doctoral students and are, instead, open to thinking through how the basic skills that have always been involved in obtaining an advanced research degree in our field can have virtually limitless application across a wide domain of careers (careers which may very well pay far better than the entry level tenure-track positions students were taught to covet). Being intentional and just a little bit creative in how we teach, supervise, and mentor these students—let alone rethinking how we talk to our undergrads about their own possible futures in academia—is what this volume is all about. And for those who are not yet persuaded by the host of programs in our field currently under threat, that have already lost their undergraduate major, or which have either merged or just closed, well, perhaps the Appendices—which provide the frank background against which the book's main chapters unfold—are the place to start this book. That I just learned that almost no one attended a panel devoted to alternative careers for students in our field, held at our November 2023 national conference in San Antonio (in which my colleague and Chair, Steven Ramey participated, what with this being a major concern to our department), tells me that a volume such as this is long overdue and, with any luck, not too late.

Russell T. McCutcheon is University Research Professor and, for 18 years, was the Chair of the Department of Religious Studies at the University of Alabama. He has written on problems in the academic labor market throughout his 30-year career and helped to design and run Alabama's skills-based M.A. in religion in culture. Among his recent work is the edited resource for instructors, *Teaching in Religious Studies and Beyond* (Bloomsbury, 2024).

Introduction

Imagine an entering cohort of eight doctoral students sitting around a table in a department seminar room or laboratory conference room. They've just arrived at graduate school, and they're eager to see what their new adventure will hold for them. All of them know that the academic job market is depressed, but most (perhaps all) are hoping for a college or university teaching job of some kind.

Now let's flash forward in time. According to current statistics, four of the eight—50%!—will not complete the degree. Of the remaining four who do finish, two will not get academic positions and will seek jobs elsewhere. The remaining pair will get full-time teaching jobs, most likely at teaching-intensive institutions. Perhaps they'll get tenure-track assistant professorships, though the supply of those positions has been shrinking. And maybe one of those two will get a position at a research university like the one where those eight students assembled years earlier.

At present there seems to be no ongoing, substantive or systematic national conversation within the academic study of religion on ways of revising doctoral programs to suit the current economic conditions of universities and colleges—conditions that have deteriorated significantly over the last decade or so, to be sure, but which have been steadily worsening for at least forty years. Referencing Leonard Cassuto and Robert Weisbuch's harsh but frank scenario quoted above, which opens their 2021 Johns Hopkins University Press book, *The New Ph.D.: How to Build a Better Graduate Education* (one among several recent volumes that the faculty of all graduate-degree granting departments in our field ought to be reading and discussing, if you ask me), few programs, if any, in our field have taken practical steps to creatively and constructively address a worsening situation that was, in fact, decades in the making (as one contributor to this volume importantly reminds us). Instead, as the epigraph to this volume makes clear (also arising from their book), anyone looking around will more than likely see that the only initiatives that often appear to be implemented are such things as increasing attention to various ways of pre-professionalizing, and thus preparing, current graduate students for academic careers (e.g., graduate programs hosting C.V. writing workshops, hosting mock on-campus interviews, encouraging publication [even if just book reviewing], facilitating teaching experience or offering pedagogy workshops, etc.) or, more drastically, just capping new enrollments in doctoral programs to accommodate declining funding opportunities on a campus or the extremely poor placement rates of such programs—if by "placement" we mean graduates landing actual tenure-track jobs, that is. (Of course, if we broaden that definition, as many programs now do, to include what often amounts to the perpetual limbo of insecure and underpaid contingent work then we may arrive at a somewhat rosier, if misleading, picture.) However, none of these responses—regardless how well-meaning such in-house and local initiatives may be or how engaged and sincere the individual faculty members who likely lead such initiatives may try to be—address the two-fold *systematic* nature of the problem: (1) the fact that many, if not most, of our field's recent, current, and at least near future doctoral students will more than likely never establish a full-time, tenure-track teaching and research career for themselves within the professorate; and (2) they are not proactively being trained by their programs in the wide relevance of the skills that they are gaining in the humanities in general and the study of religion in particular (regardless their degree level, though these are conversations some of us are at least familiar with having while trying to recruit undergraduate majors)—training in depth but also breadth that would surely help with the retention and graduation rates of such programs, by the way.

(That the American Academy of Religion [AAR] and Society of Biblical Literature [SBL]—the North American field's largest professional association—have not [as of writing these lines] produced their joint jobs report, analyzing the number and types of openings since 2019–2020 [posted June 30, 2020, well prior to the Fall 2020 hiring season, the first under COVID-19 protocols and budget cuts], is sadly representative of how the importance of this issue continues to elude us. [See Appendix 2 for more on this data.] The situation seems even bleaker when we add to this that "[a]cross all humanities departments, only 40% track career outcomes for their graduate students, and 29% reported tracking no career outcomes at all. Religion departments were even less likely to track career outcomes for their students, as 44% of departments fail to track any information about their students' outcomes. This was the second highest share in the humanities" [as reported at the close of Josh Patterson and Rob Townsend's May 2021 *Religious Studies News* report, "Engagement with the Digital, Department Life, and Professionalization"][1]—a report drawing on 2017's American Academy of Arts and Sciences' [AAAS] Humanities Indicators report, "The State of Religion Departments in Four-Year Colleges and Universities.")

Instead, on far too many campuses even today, the seemingly obvious autonomy of graduate school's outcomes seems to mirror the presumed autonomy of our field's object of study, variously known as religion, faith, experience the sacred, the holy, even meaning, let alone the countless sites where the "it" of any of these is supposedly manifested or, as some today prefer to say, embodied or materialized and thereby expressed—from scriptures and rituals to food and roadside shrines, coupled with the longstanding and cross-disciplinary privilege assumed to attend doctoral work (the so-called life of the mind approach to scholarship that has shown itself to be surprisingly resilient). Taken together this all means that programs, supervisors, and graduate advisees alike often fail to see, or even ask questions concerning, any of the wider applicability of the skills that they routinely use in their studies (e.g., definition, description, comparison, analysis [whether interpretative or explanatory], and translation, to name just a few of the more obvious ones); as the old chestnut goes, religion, being unique, requires unique interpretive methods for its study. And thus, we arrive at the highly siloed nature of a field in which being called a generalist is now a bit of a slur and specialists in this or that subfield almost never attend a conference session and rarely read or even cite a volume in any area other than their own— let alone imagine the wider applications of, let's say, the comparative method or language skills that they have worked so hard to perfect. The challenge, then, at a time when traditional academic positions have long been dwindling—to put it mildly—is how the path toward earning an advanced research degree in religious studies can be re-imagined so as to empower its graduates to be competitive for a wide variety of futures, *both within and outside of academia.* It is a reimagining that, as others have argued, does *not* require "watering down" the degree, but which does presume a willingness to work in novel and creative ways, thinking outside the box as they say, to identify the multiple (maybe even surprising) uses to which these advanced research skills can also be put—applications often unconceived by the faculty who today supervise graduate work since, given that they each won the lottery by landing their positions in doctoral programs, they probably never really had to confront such issues themselves and in their own early hunt for a career. It is also a reimagining that is not limited by the still common under-standing of the study of religion as somehow being a member of the so-called helping professions (counseling, social work, ministry, etc.), as too many career counselors on our campuses persist in assuming when they speak with our stu-dents, as if students studying religion are somehow destined for a socially ther-apeutic role. For too long this has often been the default logic when such things as service learning or so-called engaged scholarship have been entertained in our field; looking over the diverse careers in which my own department's most ded-icated students, whether undergraduate or graduate, have long been succeed-ing—everything from law and medicine to education, business, and an array of interesting staff positions on university campuses—I know that we can be far more ambitious than that. Our emphasis on thick digital skills at Alabama reflects just that ambition. But looking around I see too few departments, notably those offering doctoral degrees, pivoting in this manner.

This consequential lacuna and the way that filling it could help to strengthen this field is precisely what this volume aims to address—hoping to spark a national conversation on the future of the study of religion, i.e., the future of our students, yes, but also the future of our departments along with their current faculty and staff members (all of whom surely hope to have jobs tomorrow). For we would be naïve, if not exceedingly privileged, not to recognize that our students' successes are directly linked to our units' continued existence.

Given the very real challenges that face the higher education job market in the humanities in North America, let alone elsewhere in the world, this multi-authored volume accomplishes this by offering an account of the current situation of our field's various degree programs (including those enrolling doctoral students; see the appendices) coupled with opening reflections by three early career scholars as well as a faculty member now working in doctoral degree-granting institu-tions in the U.S. It then provides a rationale and some concrete proposals for a way forward, by way of a manifesto, which, in turn, comprises the starting point for several reflections by a collection of scholars now working in or even leading religious studies programs in the U.S. that house doctoral degrees (both public and private schools). The overall aim for the volume is therefore to move forward, on a variety of fronts, and among future, current, and recent graduate students, as well as those who now train them, a discussion on the content, process, and purpose of acquiring advanced research skills in an early twenty-first century university, one that inhabits a social, political and economic ecosystem that is rather unlike those of its predecessors. For this is a time when most everyone in higher education knows that, barring a radical change in the economy and government priorities, a decreasing few who earn doctoral degrees, in the humanities at least, will ever attain secure work as tenured faculty members, while an ever-increasing number of these students will, instead, either end up in various sorts of tenuous, contingent faculty positions (positions which, over the past decades, have increasingly populated faculty ranks on many campuses) or, for a variety of reasons, opt to seek careers well outside of academia, where the explicit relevance of their training may be uncertain if not utterly uncharted. (In fact, there are those both in and outside of academia who continue to maintain that a Ph.D. is an impediment for gaining entry into some professional settings.) The volume therefore asks what the role of these students' faculty, supervisors, degree programs, and departments ought to be in helping them—and thereby helping these doctoral programs themselves, along with their affiliated faculty members, all of whom depend upon working in viable Ph.D.-granting programs—to excel in environments that are often not kind to scholarship as well as scholars in the humanities.

While the two appendices provide necessary background data and analysis that sets the stage for the entire volume, section one provides additional context by offering the full transcripts of four exchanges first posted on my own department's podcast in September 2022 (and then later reposted on the New Books Network's site), hosted and produced by one of our then M.A. students, Erica Bennet—also involving another of our M.A. alums, Jacob Barrett (now pursuing his Ph.D. at the University of North Carolina)—in conversations with: a history Ph.D. graduate then recently on the job market; a longtime faculty member in the Department of English at the University of Florida; an English Ph.D. student who had then very recently left the degree due, in part, to his institution's lack of attention to these very issues; and a recent Ph.D. in religious studies who went on to establish a career in the tech sector. Section two comprises the co-authored manifesto on the future of graduate education in the humanities in general and the study of religion in particular (which was originally published, in the current form, in a 2023 issue of *The Bulletin for the Study of Religion*). Its authors are two tenured faculty members (one being myself) and three recent doctoral graduates in the study of religion who have each developed successful careers for themselves outside of academia. Using this manifesto as the basis, the third section of the volume—Erin Bartram's sober and, more than likely, correct comments notwithstanding (see her post, "A Profession, If You Can Keep It," cited in the

Resources section to the book)—includes solicited reflections and commentaries on the manifesto by scholars now in positions of leadership at four different U.S. doctoral programs in the study of religion (UNC, Boston, Florida State, and the University of Chicago). These respondents were all invited to comment on the manifesto by offering reflections on their own settings and/or practical steps and strategies that might be adopted locally or even widely to ensure that doctoral degrees in the humanities remain relevant, desirable to obtain, and affordable—regardless the various factors impacting academia (factors that, we must realize, no one chair, graduate director, or department as a whole, let alone college or university, can sufficiently moderate or eliminate). To better place the volume within the audience whose experiences have inspired it, the book opens with a foreword and closes with an afterword written by recent Ph.D. graduates who have both successfully carved out careers for themselves that are outside of the traditional tenure-track system.

This volume should therefore be of interest to *all* students in the study of religion, whatever the degree in which they are enrolled, but especially those who wish to imagine for themselves a future in or outside of academia where either the content or the skills of their religious studies degrees are relevant and applicable. But it is also aimed at current faculty members in the field and beyond, in particular those who are now working in either undergraduate and graduate programs and who agree that the future of the field as well as the humanities writ large (i.e., its ability to continue to support thriving doctoral degree programs as well as viable undergraduate majors) is linked to the kind of retooling supported by the volume. But it should also be of use to contingent faculty considering their own futures along with doctoral alums who have already forged careers for themselves outside of academia, inasmuch as it will at least confirm for them the challenges of their situation and, I hope, help them to celebrate their successes even though those success may have fallen well outside the so-called traditional sorts of positions and careers for which many of us hoped when we started a doctorate program. Finally, although it focuses on only one field and on the situation in U.S. higher education in particular, the widespread nature of these issues and challenges, in a wide variety of disciplines and national settings, will ensure that the volume can be seen as a case study of relevance to scholars in other humanities fields and in other national settings, where revisions to the Ph.D. are just as necessary given the widespread nature of these challenges.

In saying all of this I must add that I am not naïve to the fact that academic disciplines and institutions are often tough to change—it's like turning an aircraft carrier around, as the old saying goes. For there's considerable momentum and plenty of history driving them in their current direction—case in point: most of the really valuable social capital that people hope to accumulate in the career has long been linked to getting away from undergraduate classes and their usually heavy teaching duties and, instead, teaching less, writing more, and in the process producing doctoral students who resemble yourself, your interests, and your scholarship (ideally, one daydreams of a school of thought being established, perhaps). The likelihood of changing all that, as part of the effort to reimagine what a research degree is all about in the twenty-first century, might be slim, I realize; after all, several centuries' worth of investments and pressures have produced the contours of the institution that we call the modern research university and the highest degree that its programs grant. But pressing on despite that is what I hope this volume inspires in those who agree that this is a challenge from which we cannot afford to back away—such as those from across the university who attended a presentation in September 2023 on my campus, where Cassuto and Weisbuch spoke about their volume. Of note is that it was an audience with, predictably some would no doubt say, very few white males in attendance, despite people who look like me still having a significant presence on contemporary university campuses. Instead, those attending (by my count) were 70% women and, of the total participants, about 45% were members of racial minority groups (despite campus being, according to our in-house 2022 data, 49% male and 76% white). If we're going to change anything then persistence and persuasion are key, to bring more colleagues to the position of agreeing that we have a real problem on our hands and so attending a few workshops let alone making curricular revisions, proposing new courses, inventing internships, reconsidering the work a dissertation does in a program, as well as learning a few new supervisory skills ourselves is a pretty good use of our time.

In fact, this very book is, if nothing else, a small piece of evidence that persistence and a desire for things to be otherwise can sometimes pay off despite the pressures of the moment; for, just as it appears here, the co-written manifesto which constitutes the core of this volume was rejected out-of-hand (i.e., it was not sent out for peer review) by the editorial team when it was submitted to what at least some have long claimed to be the leading U.S. journal in our field, the *Journal of the American Academy of Religion*. The July 26, 2022, rejection email read as follows (quoting verbatim and in full):

> I'm afraid your manuscript is not suitable for publication in the *Journal of the American Academy of Religion*. After internal editorial review, we have decided not to send it to external reviewers. The paper includes no bibliography, it is not properly blinded—it identifies the authors as being at the University of Alabama—and among the scant footnotes, McCutcheon and Hughes are the only scholars put forth as visionaries. Although the topic is important and we'd like to address it in the pages of the *JAAR*, this particular paper does not substantively intervene in ongoing conversations and debates on the relevant issues.

While it should be more than obvious to readers of this volume that the manifesto is not a traditional research essay, brimming with footnotes and citations and persuasive argumentation, it seems that this was the only template that the journal's team was able to use in situating it or in understanding its possible relevance to the broad field that the journal supposedly represents. What's more, despite how important the topic apparently is, since that time, and to the best of my knowledge, that journal has not published anything in this area—no journal in the field has, in fact and the more professionally-inclined publications in the field are all but silent on it these days. But, as it turns out, I am very grateful for that editorial team's lack of imagination, shall we say, in confronting, head on, what I consider to be the most pressing problem that now confronts the entire field; for that unilateral rejection prompted the co-authors to think rather more ambitiously than just publishing an essay in a lone national journal. And thus, you have the edited book that you now hold.

Given that these challenges were all decades in the making and that no one in our field, at least as far as I can tell, is actually discussing them in any systematic or consequential form, I'll trust that the readers who find this book let alone the respondents who so kindly agreed to join this conversation will judge it rather differently than did those editors, concluding instead that it makes a substantive and relevant intervention—one that, ideally, invites others to join the conversation. That Richard Newton, my colleague and the editor of *The Bulletin for the Study of Religion* (where just the manifesto appeared in the summer of 2023), and that Janet Joyce, of Equinox Publishers (*The Bulletin*'s publisher), as well as Emily Crews, the editor for the series in which this volume appears, thought rather differently about the paper and the topic does offer us some hope for the future of the field—a future that, I sincerely believe, is in real jeopardy if it continues to get squeezed at both ends (as discussed already in the preface). For while undergraduate programs are merged, cut, or at the very least are undermined by systematic attacks on the humanities (whether rhetorical or budgetary, even including nation-wide revisions in the U.S. to so-called general education requirements), shrinking hiring budgets across the nation's universities place in peril the (now meagre, I admit) hope of work as a faculty member for our doctoral graduates (the very people whose labor as teaching assistants or even instructors of record generates the undergraduate credit hour production that helps us to justify the existence of our departments). I would hope that those already working in the field and in positions of leadership throughout it—especially the members of a generation of scholars younger than my own—will, sooner or later, come to see that tackling all of this as not only being their responsibility but also in their own best interest, since, at the end of the day, it is the future of their own positions and their own departments that are at risk. That sooner would be better than later should be obvious, what with the number of departments of religious studies that have already been either eliminated or collapsed into a curiously named cross-disciplinary unit.

Whether you work in a doctoral program or a small liberal arts college, have tenure or a short-term contract, whether you are an undergrad or a graduate student, or if you have already left academia behind you but retain a nostalgia for the subject matter that once occupied so much of your time, my hope is that you will find something of use in this volume. But more than this: my hope is also that you will come up with some good ideas of your own and be invested enough to engage in the sort of collaborative action needed to address these challenges and implement some revisions. For the optimist in me—and, as I've written before, what else is a critic but someone who thinks that things could be far better than they now are—can see a reimagined field in the near future, with creatively revised requirements and more explicit skill acquisition, that thrives in a way that our current departments clearly do not. Realizing that vision will be labor intensive, to be sure, but of benefit to us all.

Russell T. McCutcheon is University Research Professor and, for 18 years, was the Chair of the Department of Religious Studies at the University of Alabama. He has written on problems in the academic labor market throughout his 30-year career and helped to design and run Alabama's skills-based M.A. in religion in culture. Among his recent work is the edited resource for instructors, *Teaching in Religious Studies and Beyond* (Bloomsbury, 2024).

Note

1   Find this report at https://rsn.aarweb.org/engagement-digital-department-life -and-professionalization (accessed May 24, 2023).

Context

Chapter 1

"The University Absolutely Had Nothing in Place ...": Life After Grad School with Bradley Sommer

Jacob Barrett, Erica Bennett, and Bradley J. Sommer

The following transcript is from the first episode of a four-part series on the University of Alabama's Study Religion podcast. The podcast was originally posted on September 6, 2022; it was hosted and produced by Erica Bennett while the transcript was produced by Erica and Jacob Barrett, now in his Ph.D. at the University of North Carolina at Chapel Hill. The guest is Bradley Sommer.

ERICA BENNETT: I am a current student in the Religion *in* Culture Master's program at the University of Alabama. As I finish up my last year of graduate school, I have tried to prepare myself for a life outside of the academic system. I do not plan to go into a Ph.D. program at the time being, so I have started to redescribe the skills I have gained during my master's program to better reflect what my future employers will look for. I have turned my C.V. into a resume, I am looking into job search websites to understand how to describe the skills I already have, and I am talking with professionals outside of academia to understand what will be expected of me.

The fact that I am even aware and thinking about these things means that I am in a position of privilege compared to many of my fellow humanities graduates. Many students in the humanities go into a Ph.D. program only to be entirely unprepared for the job market after they receive their degree. This is true whether they want to be professors in a field with only one tenure track position open nationwide or they want to transition into a non-academic career path but have little to no understanding of that job market.

What is the job market really like for recent graduates? How can students be more prepared for a life after their studies? How can already existing institutions tweak their approaches to further help not only those becoming professors, but all of their graduates? And is it still advantageous to get a doctoral degree in the humanities? In this special four-part series, I will be talking with recent UA graduate, Jacob Barrett, about his worries on starting a Ph.D. program. We will be listening to interviews from a variety of voices in the academic community to help flesh out the answers to these questions. Higher education must figure out what students, faculty, and institutions can do to remedy these problems and how to better prepare for jobs outside of academia, and this series aims to explore such remedies.

* * *

ERICA BENNETT: Hi Jacob. You are starting classes for your Ph.D. program in religious studies at the University of North Carolina at Chapel Hill soon, right?

JACOB BARRETT: I am, and I am excited but also a little nervous. I have gotten a lot of advice from different faculty about pursuing a career in academia and continuing my education in a Ph.D. program, and I keep seeing conversations all over Twitter that make me a little worried about what comes after a Ph.D. program given the state of the academic job market. I have seen tweet after tweet from people who have just completed their Ph.D.s and can't find jobs in their field. Even outside of academia they seem to be struggling to find jobs. So, I am a little worried I will fall in the same boat and I just want to be prepared when I get to the end of my program for whatever that looks like. I want to know a little more about what is going on, what is happening with graduate programs in the humanities, and if there is anything I can do now to prepare for succeeding in the future.

ERICA BENNETT: That does sound really worrisome, Jacob. I bet, though, that people would be willing to talk to us and explain a little more about what they have been tweeting. Is there any tweet in particular that has caused some worry?

JACOB BARRETT: I saw one the other day from Bradley Sommer that read:

> Okay tweeps. I need help. Those of you with Ph.D.s who are not in academia but have jobs which require/utilize your Ph.D. skills, can you tell me (here or DM): (1) how you found it, (2) how you got it, and (3) where I should be looking. Bonus: maybe let me know if you hear anything?

ERICA BENNETT: I saw that tweet too. Why don't I just call him and have a discussion with him about the tweet and where he is after his Ph.D. program? Maybe that will give you a little less worry.

JACOB BARRETT: Yes, that sounds great! Thank you, Erica!

* * *

ERICA BENNETT: Would you explain a little about the tweet and the context that it came from?

BRADLEY J. SOMMER: I can't remember what specific job I had been just rejected from, but there was a job that I had applied for. I interviewed a couple of times, felt fairly confident about my chances, and then got that sort of universal email of, "You were great. You were grand. You were wonderful. But we're going with somebody else for X, Y, Z reasons." And I was kind of frustrated because at that point, even though I had only graduated in May of last year, I had functionally been on the job market since about February or March of the year before once my dissertation was essentially done. Especially once I had defended, my advisor told me to go ahead and start applying for things because if anyone asked, he would say, "Brad is on track to graduate."

I had known for a while that I probably was not going to find a job in academia because of the way academia is right now. I had applied for a few academic things, a couple post-doctoral fellowships, one full time but not tenure track teaching job, but by and large everything else I had applied for—and this is still the case now—has been outside of academia, whether it's academia adjacent like working for a nonprofit higher education sort of organization or something that is not in academia at all. The problem is that I had no prior training, preparation, or understanding of what that world is actually like.

And so if success is being defined as having a job right now, then I'm not successful and no one's successful until they get a job. If you measure success, though, by getting a little bit better at the process, getting more feedback, and getting more callbacks, I've been more successful. But early on, I was having very little success because I was not prepared to apply to non-academic jobs. I knew that you do not just send a C.V. to a non-academic job because they are not going to read an eight-page C.V. At the same time, I also kind of thought that if I took my C.V. and had a truncated version that hit the high points and then a cover letter that was like, "Hey, look at me, I'm great, grand, and wonderful. I have these abilities and this education" that I would have a lot more success. And I wasn't really having success. When I posted that tweet, the frustration was coming from a place where I felt like I had been doing a lot of the things that I had been told to do but I still was not really getting a lot of practical success. I was getting some interviews, but not a ton. I had been offered two things that I had to turn down because they simply didn't pay enough.

That was the rationale for the tweet. I wanted to know how people found what they found, because there are so many opportunities out there for folks coming out of graduate school, whether they are coming out with a Ph.D., a master's of some variety, a law degree and maybe they do not want to practice, and so on. There are a lot of options, but knowing where to find them is really, really hard, especially if you are in certain fields. But then I also wanted to ask how people got the jobs they did because there are a lot of things that you do when you're in graduate school that you do not realize have real world applications or you do not know how to articulate them into the real world. You only know how to describe them in the academic context. So, the tweet was trying to basically get people who successfully were able to make that transition—whether it was right out of graduate school or if they had worked for a while doing something in academia before transitioning—to talk about how they found the job that they have, the first job that they got, the kind of skills they had, where they looked for these jobs, who they talked to, and so on because I don't think really anything is being done to help graduate students, or even recent graduates in certain disciplines, get into the jobs that are available which are, more often than not, not in academia.

ERICA BENNETT: What I'm hearing you say is that most of the tweet came from this frustration of knowing you have the skills but lacking the resources and preparation to transition into a non-academic job market successfully, and this kind of frustration leads you to the open forum of Twitter trying your best to just get this transition right.

BRADLEY J. SOMMER: Exactly. Let me give you an example. There was a job that I applied for that was a research heavy job at a sort of active think tank that was in an area of my expertise. It was in labor and urban policy, so it was kind of a perfect match. They wanted somebody with advanced degree experience, so I figured applying for this job I could just be like, "Well I have a Ph.D. in history, specializing in these things, I wrote a dissertation, blah, blah, blah." I got a preliminary interview, which is something that happens a lot for these industry jobs where it's not an interview with the company, but it might be an interview with a subcontracted HR department. One of the first questions they asked me was, "Why is a history professor applying for this research heavy position?"

I was really taken aback by the question because I was like, "Well, I'm not a professor. I just graduated and you can see that I haven't been a professor." But I answered the question with, "Well, you know, a Ph.D.'s a research degree." And they were like, "In what way? Can you explain that?" I was really taken aback because they were not asking me to see if I could answer the question. I think this person truly did not realize that a Ph.D. was a research degree and that a dissertation is an original research project. It's the equivalent of writing a book which we—people in graduate school and in academia—know that, but not everybody knows that. So, even just translating the academic experience into the non-academic world has been really, really tricky. I am learning how to take my academic experiences and translate them into something that makes sense in the non-academic world, and it's only been in the last two or three months that I can finally speak the correct verbiage to get people to understand what I'm saying.

ERICA BENNETT: When you were going through your Ph.D. program, were you preparing for these struggles afterwards? In other words, when you were fully in the academic system, were you prepared for the job market that you were shot into?

BRADLEY J. SOMMER: Yes and no. I knew that it was going to be a tough academic job market and I had known that for a while. I am 32 years old, so I've lived through several once-in-a-generation economic collapses at this point, and I knew that there were not going to be a ton of academic jobs. Even once I decided to go for my master's degree, I knew I probably was going to do something else. I did not know exactly what, but I knew it was probably not going to be academia, at least probably not right off the bat. I had started preparing in sort of subtle ways. I got really involved in a higher education nonprofit that is organized for and by graduate and professional students. Through that, I met a lot of people who work in other higher education nonprofit organizations. I networked a little bit doing that and I leaned on those people a lot the closer I got to graduation, asking what things I could be doing, who I should talk to, what organizations I should consider, and so on. That was helpful to a certain degree, but I also was not prepared because I had a lot of misconceptions about pursuing a non-academic career track that I had to find out on my own.

ERICA BENNETT: Did your program prepare you for this job market or what did you do to prepare for this?

BRADLEY J. SOMMER: My program was a traditional program in the sense that it was structured with two years of coursework, doctoral exams, prospectus, and then you are ABD, and you are just researching and writing your dissertation. My cohort was I think the last or second-to-last cohort that had that. A year or two after I did my exams, Carnegie Mellon's history department rebranded, and it restructured their program. Now, it's no longer geared so heavily towards the exams because the exam system is really for those people going into academia. I do not know exactly what they have now, I think it's some kind of portfolio project that encompasses a lot, but at the time they were not really doing anything systemically or even on a one-to-one basis to really help us go into non-academic careers.

The people who were in our program who got non-academic jobs either knew somebody from before they were in graduate school or just sort of stumbled into the jobs. During the course of doing their dissertation, they just connected with somebody who was like, "Hey, you're great. When you graduate, do you want to come work here?" And then they did. Systemically, the department did not have anything in place. The university absolutely had nothing in place. If you were not a graduate student in robotics, machine learning, engineering, etc. there were no viable career placement services for you. There are people you can call, but they did not really have a whole lot of advice other than to go on Indeed to look for jobs.

ERICA BENNETT: Do you think academia as a whole is preparing students for a life outside the academic system?

BRADLEY J. SOMMER: No. Categorically no. Let me caveat that: there are disciplines within academia where there are resources for students who are transitioning out of their programs, whether it's because they are graduating or maybe they just were able to get hired with their existing credentials. Most professional degree programs already have things built into them to do that sort of preparation. So, if someone is a lawyer or a medical doctor or has an M.B.A., those programs have that kind of support structured into them. If you are a law student, in the summer between year two and year three you go and work at a firm and you get some experience. If you do well, you probably get an offer to work for them after you graduate and pass the bar. If nothing else, maybe you can get a recommendation from them for somewhere else. In medical school, they have that whole placement system. Public policy and M.B.A. students have a lot of internship opportunities as part of their program. Being at a tech-heavy school, there would be job fairs on campus where a lot of tech companies would come, and they would set up booths like a high school science fair. You would just walk around and talk to those recruiters, and they would try and get you to come work for Facebook for a year after you graduate because after a year you would get a job offer to make a hefty six figures and you'll be, you'll be good. That is overwhelmingly not the case in a lot of the "traditional" academic disciplines.

Within history, religious studies, literature, languages, and other disciplines, everyone knows that we are not getting hired into academic jobs. Unless you are a Ph.D. student at an Ivy League school or one of the three or four schools that are directly beneath the Ivy League in your respective field, you are probably not going into a full tenure-track academic job. Everybody in academia knows that, but people outside of academia, I don't think realize that as much, which I think is why I got that question from that HR person about why a history professor was applying for a job.

There is sort of the conflation of "Ph.D." with "professor" but one's a degree and one is a job title. While they generally overlap, they are not synonyms. So, I think that a lot of people, especially people who are in the hiring industry, don't realize that there are people with graduate degrees not going into academia with a lot of easily transferable skills. I think a lot of people look at somebody with a Ph.D. in engineering or in a hard science and might say, "Oh, well there is a very clear industry for something like that." I don't know that people look at history or religious studies or languages and say the same thing. There is not a history factory that I can go work at and make the history. There's not some super prestigious government lab where I go down into the archives and just sit and muse about things while looking over ancient scrolls. There is a bit of a clash between the internal knowing of what is going on within academia and the sort of external expectation of what graduate students are doing when they graduate.

Both I think are partly to blame but, if I'm going to be completely honest, I think the larger share of the blame falls on the academy. I think it is great when senior tenured faculty will go online and lament the decline of academia and how the discipline is going to cease to exist. But I can't help but think, "Wow, man, if only you were the person in charge who could make the changes to make this happen. If only I was a 70-year-old tenured professor with all kinds of clout and authority, and if only I was the department head and could make these changes." I think a lot of the blame is in academia. Some of that blame is internal to departments. Some of it is also at the university level. I do think that a non-insignificant number of university presidents and chancellors still labor under this pretense that Ph.D.s are just walking into full-time academic jobs. So, I would say that academia as a whole is absolutely not doing enough to help us transition into the jobs that are available.

Frankly, when there are full-time tenure track job postings, a lot of people don't want to apply for them. They do because they need to have a job, but there is almost a sort of sense of relief. It's like, "Whew, I didn't have to go be a professor at that university and labor for years to try and actually get tenure and then not even make a whole lot of money or maybe have to move to a state that socially and politically might not be the best situation for me." There are a lot of problems within academia around the issue of graduate students getting jobs.

ERICA BENNETT: What would be one piece of advice that you wish you had heard before entering graduate school?

BRADLEY J. SOMMER: I wish somebody would have told me in a practical way and not in a scare tactic way that I probably was not going to go into academia. I knew, but it's one thing to have your suspicions and it's another thing to have somebody make eye contact with you and tell you that you are not going into academia. I have no problem being blunt and telling people that it's a really hard job market right now and that, if they go to graduate school, they probably will not go into academia. I would also be blunt and say that if someone is going to go into a Ph.D. program, specifically start talking to people and start looking into the kinds of jobs that you think you might want to do now. Try and contact people who graduated from your program that you are going into and see where they ended up.

That said, I am never going to yell at somebody who wants to go to graduate school and tell them not to. If they have the opportunity, I am not going to make an assessment on somebody's ability to go to graduate school in terms of the time, money, funding, and so on available to them. I get annoyed when people will just flat out say, "Don't go to graduate school. Drop out of your program," because a lot of the times the people that are saying that are people who have tenure-track jobs who went to Harvard and their parents were professors. How dare you tell somebody to not pursue an education, especially if they are somebody who is first generation or if they are going into a field where there is a history of marginalization of certain communities like communities of color, women, queer people, and so on. I'm a queer person who is one of the first people in my family to go to graduate school, so how dare you tell somebody to not get an education. The people who phrase it that way, to use the parlance of the youth, can miss me with that nonsense. I have no time for that argument. I think it's disingenuous. I think it's hypocritical. If that is the advice that somebody has for somebody, they probably should not be in academia because they are clearly part of the problem.

I have no problem, though, giving people directions on how to look for non-academic jobs, the kind of job titles they should look for, and the kind of organizations they should look for. That, I think, is way more constructive. I hate when people fall into the trap of blaming the students because it is not the students' problem. I see this a lot on social media or every now and then in some poorly constructed New York Times think piece where someone will be like, "Well, academia should be taking fewer students since there's fewer academic jobs." And that is also not the answer because while there are fewer academic jobs for sure, there are not fewer places for those people to go. They just don't know how to get to those places.

Rather than say, "Hey Alabama, don't take as many students," say, "Hey Alabama, here are some resources that you can implement into your program, top down and systemically." To help your students go into the places where they are likely to get hired, here is how to help them develop the networks that they need, the skill sets that they need, and here is how to help them translate their university experience into real world experience. I think that is a way better use of time than telling someone that they should not go to graduate school.

I went to school to get this degree and get this skill set. The job I get can be a professor position, but it doesn't have to be. There is a lot of pressure to want to go into academia when you have been in academia, and it is really easy to get this sort of retroactive imposter syndrome. You look around and see someone else who has a Ph.D. with a super fancy job as a professor at such and such university, and you are an analyst for a research company with the same Ph.D. There is a social pressure to think that you are not as much of a Ph.D. as that other person because your Ph.D. is not being used as much as theirs is. Sometimes we put that sort of pressure on ourselves, and I think sometimes people in our social circles who don't know what it's like can also put that pressure on us. I think that's part of the problem too. There needs to be less of an assumption about what you can and cannot do with a Ph.D., and I think that that's a conversation that more people need to have.

* * *

ERICA BENNETT: Jacob, I spoke with Bradley and, as you heard, we really talked about his journey outside of getting his Ph.D. We talked about how prepared he felt while in his Ph.D. for the job market he was entering, and then we talked about what skills or opportunities he wished he had had in the Ph.D. program to better prepare him for his life now. Our conversation was mostly an overview of where higher education institutions are failing to help their students succeed.

JACOB BARRETT: I really liked what Bradley had to say about the breakdown between the individual support he received and the institutional support that was there, or more accurately was not there. It sounds like the faculty that he was working with and his network that he had built were giving him really good advice, but one of the bigger problems that he saw and experienced was that there was not this institutional level of support from the university.

ERICA BENNETT: Talking with Bradley really helped me understand not only the motivation behind his tweet but probably why lots of people in academia are tweeting about the job market. It seems to be mostly out of frustration and almost desperation for help. People are looking for any help they can get, and Twitter is their last-ditch effort. I think after talking with Bradley, we kind of understand the base issues that are facing humanities graduates.

JACOB BARRETT: I think it would be really interesting to see what someone on the faculty side of things who might be trying to offer that sort of individual support to make up for the lack of institutional support has to say about this problem.

ERICA BENNETT: Definitely. Maybe we can look back on Twitter. I saw that there were a ton of responses to Bradley's original tweet and I see one in particular from Pamela Gilbert, an English professor at the University of Florida. Let me talk with her to understand what faculty are doing to aid their students and what she has experienced in her years in the academy regarding the job market.

Jacob Barrett is a Ph.D. student in the Department of Religious Studies at the University of North Carolina at Chapel Hill, interested in questions about religion and governance, law, and the state. He hosts at the New Books Network Podcast and works as the Marketing and Communications Coordinator for both the North American Association for the Study of Religion (NAASR) and the American Academy of Religion Southeast region (AAR-SE).

Erica Bennett received her B.A. in Religious Studies at Millsaps College and her M.A. in Religious Studies from the University of Alabama. She spent much of her college career developing skills in research, museum studies, and podcasting/digital creation; she now works full-time as an Event Coordinator for the University of Alabama.

Bradley J. Sommer earned his Ph.D. in American History from Carnegie Mellon University and is a historian at the U.S. Army Center of Military History in Washington, D.C. He is also an online adjunct professor at Miami University in Ohio. Currently, he is working on a book about Toledo, OH, in the latter half of the twentieth century, entitled *Tomorrow Never Came: Toledo, Ohio and the Making of Postindustrial Midwest.*

Chapter 2

"A Series of Decisions Which Are Going to Affect You Over Time …": Life After Grad School with Pamela Gilbert

Jacob Barrett, Erica Bennett, and Pamela K. Gilbert

The following transcript is from the second episode of a four-part series on the University of Alabama's Study Religion podcast. The podcast was originally posted on September 6, 2022; it was hosted and produced by Erica Bennett while the transcript was produced by Erica and Jacob Barrett, now in his Ph.D. at the University of North Carolina at Chapel Hill. The guest is Pamela Gilbert.

ERICA BENNETT: My name is Erica Bennett and I am a current student in the Religion *in* Culture Master's program at the University of Alabama. This is the second episode in a special series on the academic job market after graduate school in the humanities. In this episode, we dive deeper into the problems facing the academic job market with Pamela Gilbert, a professor from the University of Florida.

* * *

PAMELA K. GILBERT: I am the Albert Brick Professor of English at the University of Florida. I specialize in nineteenth-century British literature and I do a lot with history of the body and history of medicine. I came on the market for the first time in the early 1990s, and actually then it was a bad market. It's worse now, but the sort of long-standing practice of relying on precarious employment has been going on for a while. In fact, I was a freeway flyer during my entire Ph.D. because, of course, I did my Ph.D. in Los Angeles and it was expensive and you couldn't possibly live on a graduate student stipend and so you cobbled things together. We all did really. I took my first position at the University of Wisconsin–Parkside, which is a branch campus of the state university and is a four-year campus. I was there from 1993 to 1997 and then I came to the University of Florida and this will be my 25th year here.

ERICA BENNETT: You had commented on a tweet by Bradley Sommer and then a response by Russell McCutcheon, and so that is how we knew to contact you. Your response to the tweet was that faculty have this important responsibility in mentoring students, but they remain removed and kind of outside of the current job market outside of academia. Why do you think that is?

PAMELA K. GILBERT: The simple answer is that even with the best intentions in the world, this is my 25th year here. I haven't been on the job market for 25 years and, even though I have interviewed for various positions, at my stage it's very different. People are looking at me for chairships or deanships or director-ships and it's a completely different skill set that they are looking at. So that's part of it. Part of it is that if you have worked for decades in one employment context, you are not going to know a lot about other employment contexts. Another problem is that, for example, after the 2008 crash, we did not hire for several years and so we did not have any people who had gone through the market recently. Now we have some, and so that has been huge for us and they have been really significant in helping us to mentor people. But again, they are coming into a higher education context from a higher education context, so they have not, for the most part, had that kind of experience either.

Where I have gone to try to understand more about what people are doing is to my own students who have done other things. Most of them are in higher education in a range of positions. Some of them are in permanent lecture-ships where they have continuing employment but they are not on the tenure track, some of them are tenure track, and some of them have decided to leave the tenure track because it wasn't giving them what they wanted in terms of opportunities for their partner or whatnot. Several have gone on in private secondary education, and I have to say their starting salaries and benefits are much better than most of the people who have gone on in higher education. Some have gone on in instructional design. One person decided she just did not even want to look in higher education, not because of the job market—because she is actually very good at it—but she didn't love teaching and if you don't love teaching this is really not the job for you. So, she's building a career doing publicity and she graduated very recently. So, what I have tried to do is put students in touch with my own network of graduate students to explore these things. I have encouraged them to do informational interviews with former students of mine. I ask my students now to really think about what they want to do. What are you good at doing? What do you love about this? What are other things that will allow you to do those things? What would a resume look like that would highlight those strengths in a way that would be appealing outside of the university?

To some extent I have had luck with referring students to the campus career centers, but they are not great with dealing with people who are moving from the academic track. They really aren't. They don't understand it, but they have been able to connect some students with other people who have gone into various other positions. I encourage them to use their other networks, and to get a LinkedIn account because apparently that's a thing. So, I try to gather the information I have from my informants that are out there and pass on that information to them. The other thing that I would say is that there are tons of jobs in community college situations. I taught in a community college over 30 years ago, but of course the job process and what they look for has changed. The flooding of the market with Ph.D.s has upped the ante for everyone. So even there, you really need to talk to people who are in those positions to understand what those job committees are looking for. It's a completely different process and different things should be highlighted in your letters. Faculty don't always know that. I have the good fortune of having worked with a lot of students, and so I can contact them and say, "I have someone who's interested. Do you have any sample letters?" but not everybody has that network.

ERICA BENNETT: You are clearly working really hard for the students that you have and who are coming to you, but that clearly indicates a disconnect between the individual support offered and the departmental and institutional support. What do you think could help change that disconnect?

PAMELA K. GILBERT: I think there are a couple of things I would say. I would say that our department is working very hard and much more effectively than in the past to address this. We have done it in part because of the advantage of having Zoom and the fact that you can contact alumni and have them Zoom in to give a presentation to your current students who are on the market. Whereas before, it was like, "Let's take our non-existent budget and try to get someone to come back and talk to people." So, my department is working very hard to do that, and I have junior colleagues who have really revolutionized our program to encourage students to think about the job market earlier and to think about shaping their experience for the job market. So, I wouldn't say that necessarily it's a disconnect between departments and individual faculty. But it is true that English is a diverse enough field that my ability to mentor people in my field has limits. We graduate film studies Ph.D.s here, and my ability to mentor them is limited. I have to say most of them are mentoring themselves better than I could anyway—I get mentored a lot by my graduate students in terms of the job market.

One thing that I have seen that I think is really encouraging is that professional organizations are really stepping up. The Modern Language Association (MLA) has taken on some of these duties, but again, they're a huge tent and there's only so much that they can do. I belong to an organization called the North American Victorian Studies Association, and over the last decade and some odd years, they have added a professionalization seminar that covers everything from the job market to grants to networking. A lot of students don't know how to network. I certainly didn't. I was a first-generation student. I had no idea how to do it, and nobody in my department told me it was important or taught me how to do it. So, we have tried to do more of that. And social media does make that more possible than it was when I was coming up, so that has been very helpful, especially in eras where lots of people do not have travel budgets. This kind of opportunity to network online, to network on Zoom, and to attend things virtually allows people access in a way that many people otherwise would never have. I'll add one more thing. One thing that our organization is experimenting with is, as part of our national meeting, we would pair one graduate student with one senior scholar from a different institution. They would read some of your stuff and give you feedback and the idea was to build a kind of connection where someone might be able to write for you or give you advice from a different standpoint.

This is a little bit sideways from what we are discussing, but one thing that has always been a problem in the academy is that Ph.D. students tend to do their Ph.D.s at R1 and R2 institutions because that's the nature of the beast. That's where Ph.D. programs are, but academia is a pyramid, and most jobs are not in those kinds of institutions. For a long time, it was kind of assumed that you would figure it out. First of all, that was never true. Secondly, it's a sort of bad model. I think that many institutions, not all, but many institutions are now doing a little bit better of a job mentoring people for positions in institutions that are not like their own, but there again, faculty ability to do that is limited because this is the water that this fish swims in. You don't know what you don't know. I have taught at a variety of institutions, but it has been many years. Some people got their first job and sort of stayed in that lane.

I see very often graduate students will get a chance to teach an upper division class and they are so excited and then they say, "Oh my God, there are 35 students in this class," because they're used to teaching the writing classes which are kept smaller. I am teaching two classes, but most people are teaching four classes. Some are teaching five and six. Some are teaching three. But it is rare that you will be teaching only two classes, let alone one class unless you landed a job at an R1. But even when I was on the market, I worked my way to an R1 job, but I also got lucky. You can work very hard and not hit that moment where the job opens for you. So, that's something that people need to think about both in terms of, "Is this the life I want?" but also in terms of, "What skills am I building to be able to manage a full workload of teaching and still be able to do the things that I need to do for the institution?" Then when you layer in the institution and its demands, very often there is the feeling that you are kind of slogging up a hill that no one wants you to get to the top of anyway. That can feel demoralizing, and it can also absorb an enormous amount of time. So yes, we all love the life of the mind, but the idea that we are going to be able to have long hours at the library and think deep thoughts is a sort of fantasy. Of course, you can have some of that, but that's not going to be your daily life.

ERICA BENNETT: As we have been talking about, the market has changed since you were on it, but not much. What was a piece of advice that you wish you would have heard going into your graduate studies? What piece of advice do you try to give those who are thinking about going into graduate school?

PAMELA K. GILBERT: I thought hard about this, and this was surprisingly difficult for me. When I was thinking of my career and what I wanted to do, I was very focused on the university. I believed that that was the place where you did the thing I wanted to do. That was largely true, but I wish that someone had told me to think about the things that I wanted to do in broader terms. To think about how this is not the only institution out there where I could use some of the skills and talents we associate with being at the university. When people are coming to me for the first time, I talk to them about how difficult the job market is. I try because a couple of people had this talk with me and, of course, I assumed it was them telling me that they thought I couldn't do it. They didn't hear the "It's not about you" part. So, I do try to say, "Let me tell you that I thought this, and I'm really not saying that this is about you." I tell them, "Don't go on unless you are basically willing to just do it anyway, because it may not lead to a career path in the university." I also tell them what I think most young people don't understand, and I certainly didn't, is that this is going to have an economic effect for the rest of your life. I'm not complaining because I have ultimately I had a soft landing. But, I tell them, "You are giving up many, many years where other people your age are entering the job market, and they are going to build wealth over those, let's say, seven years. And you are still going to be at zero or below zero having taken on more debt. That is wealth that you are not putting away. It's not just that you are not earning that wealth, it's a deficit that rolls out for the rest of your life." And it is not an easy lateral move when you enter the market if you decide to leave academia. They are comparing you to 21- and 22-year-olds, and they are looking at you and thinking, "Well, those people are cheaper. I can train them. They're going to be less demanding because they're just getting started. I can mold them." That's a real issue.

I think a lot of people want to do some graduate work or are interested in pursuing things but are seeing it's a bad market and they're thinking, "Why do I want to go out there now?" An M.A. degree is a completely different animal than a Ph.D. An M.A. kind of allows you to explore those things and maybe have the teaching experience and see what you think of it. It doesn't really cost you that much provided you don't, you know, stupidly go into a lot of debt, because those two years are not going to make a radical difference. But the time that you put into a Ph.D. is a real commitment. I mean, we do talk about the fact that there are fungible skills and abilities that will be respected in other domains, and that is absolutely true. But the reality is that you're spending many years training to do something specific, and if you are not doing that specific thing, then you have lost something in terms of economic progress. I took a huge pay cut to take my first full-time job because I was teaching four to six courses a semester as a freeway flyer, and I took a $10,000 a year pay cut to take a job in a place that I didn't particularly want to move to because it was a career move. I'm very lucky to have had the opportunity to do that. I'm not complaining, but again, all along the way is a series of decisions which are going to affect you over time, and which are going to affect your income over time. That may feel unimportant when you're in your twenties. It might feel more important if you have a child, or perhaps a child with special needs. It might feel more important if your parents get sick and suddenly need you to support them. A lot of life happens in those seven to ten years, and things can change on the ground a lot.

The wisdom, as long as I've been in this career, is you go wherever the job is. You are not going to be able to stay where you are. You have to be willing to go anywhere, and that is still essentially true. I really think people need to think about what's important to them because first having a tenure track job at a not great university may be an unacceptable sacrifice. I just had a former student of mine leave a tenured full professorship, and she was just done with living there. It was a good job, and she didn't hate her colleagues. They valued her, but she just wanted to be in a different place, and she couldn't do that. She couldn't make it work. So, she left. She's working for an NGO now and she's very happy. That is a valid decision. I had students that I had great hopes for and I thought that they could have a research career and do the whole tenure track thing. They were well positioned for it, but the reality was, "It is important to me to be by my family in Miami," and, "I have kids and I want them to know their grandparents," and, "My partner needs this job." All of those are real valid reasons to make choices, and you shouldn't feel influenced by anything other than your own priorities because this career does not reward you enough in other ways to compensate you for what you will lose.

ERICA BENNETT: That's really great advice. I think that kind of advice could apply even outside of academia, but I think that's really good advice especially for those who are seeking academic success. My last question is if you think humanities programs are preparing students for jobs outside of academia.

PAMELA K. GILBERT: Undergraduate programs are doing a great job preparing students for a wide range of careers. We see that in terms of their lifetime earnings and work experience because they actually eventually do better than a lot of people in more technical fields who may place at higher earning jobs immediately out of college and then stagnate. If you want to take a couple of years to really deeply explore a topic, I think that the M.A. is still an acceptable trade off because you will learn things. Especially if you take advantage of all the opportunities to work with digital things and take advantage of all of those things that are going on at the university. The M.A. is great with the things that maybe you feel a little uncomfortable with. The whole point of higher education is that you can take some risks and get a little uncomfortable.

The Ph.D., as it stands, is not doing a fabulous job preparing people for positions outside of academia. It's not designed to do that. I know people have talked about how we could change it. Many years ago, the MLA tried to promote a different kind of doctoral degree that would be more skills focused on a wide range of skills, and people didn't want it. People tend to want to go into the humanities because they want to study deeply and immerse themselves in the scholarship on the questions about human values and how humans make meaning. I think that that's well worth doing, but you shouldn't go into it with your eyes closed. You shouldn't go into it thinking that there is a clear career path, because at this point in history, there is not.

To some extent, it was never true that everyone who did a dissertation was then going to spend the rest of their life doing that kind of work. They were going to go and teach a four-four and administer and serve the community in that way. The Ph.D. prepares you for that in the sense that you are a member of the academic community, and you know what it is to create a contribution to knowledge which is what graduate work is supposed to be. So that is a valid preparation even if you don't spend the rest of your career doing that all the time. There's still a need for education, which means that there should still be lots of full-time jobs in education.

The reason that there are not is an economic structure. It's not that there's a shortage of need. If there were a shortage of need, we wouldn't be hiring a bunch of adjuncts or very poorly paid lecturers. I will say that a lot of institutions are making progress with having sort of dual tracks where teaching track positions are full time with some protection and some permanency built into them. We've done that here at UF. So, I mean, there are ways that some improvements are happening, but it's not enough and it's not widespread enough.

I think honestly that the most important thing academics can do is join a union. Be part of a union. Collectively bargain. I'm in a right to work state, so I'm in a union that doesn't have a lot of legal power and yet it does a lot for us. It does a lot to maneuver, and I think that's very important because the casualization of labor has been going on for a hell of a long time. Like I said, I was a freeway flyer when I was working on my Ph.D. and I had no illusions about the market because even though I had faculty who had placed back in the sixties and had no idea what the market was like, I looked at my peers who were really good and they were working on three campuses and not having a permanent job. I knew that that was a possibility for me too, right from the jump. I don't mean to minimize the fact that things are much worse today, but this has been a long-term strategy of the entire economic system. It's become untenable. It's been untenable for a while, and I don't see any way out of that except collective bargaining and making different laws to protect people and so on.

ERICA BENNETT: I think it's easy to fall into the trap of thinking, "It's just me. It's just our generation. It's just my problem." So, it's nice to see—well not nice—but it's good to hear that this isn't just a recent issue. We need to look at the deeper reasons why this has been happening because, like you said, it didn't just start yesterday. There are a lot of things that were put into place or not put into place that really lead us to this moment.

PAMELA K. GILBERT: That is absolutely true. Higher Education has been in crisis. Labor has been in crisis. That's been true for a while, but the political moment right now is the worst I've seen in my lifetime and probably the worst that we've seen since maybe the 1920s. Obviously there's the labor front and there's the institutional reform front, but I think that people really need to think through their political choices. They need to be politically active at the local level and not just at the national level because freedom of speech is under threat. Academic freedom is under threat. Tenure is under threat, but more importantly, the institution of higher education, as we know it as a place where we explore ideas as a place where not everything has to be driven by a profit, is at an inflection point. Either we are going to save it, or it is not going to exist in a decade or so except for maybe in very few elite institutions for wealthy people. That's the question underlying all of this, and it's not unrelated to the economic and labor questions we're talking about.

* * *

JACOB BARRETT: It was so great hearing from Pamela. I really enjoyed what she had to say about how the problem of the job market is not a new problem and that it's something that she remembers hearing about and experiencing when she first went on the job market. I think that was really interesting to hear about because we talk about it so much as a problem right now that is this new thing, but it sounds like from what Pamela was saying that this is a problem that's been around for years. I guess it's interesting to me that it's still a problem and that we haven't really figured out how to fix it and navigate it completely.

ERICA BENNETT: I really liked talking with Pamela as well because she helped shed a light on how faculty members are, in most cases, doing all they can. They are doing what they can with the resources that they have for their students, that they have under their wing. I think that's probably true for most faculty members. I think the issue comes when we ask people within the academic system to help those leaving the academic world. So few of those getting doctorates are landing tenure track positions and programs are in trouble. The students leaving the humanities are not prepared for the job market and their advisors and colleges are not preparing them for a job outside of the academic system. It has left many students reconsidering their degrees in the middle of their programs.

Jacob Barrett is a Ph.D. student in the Department of Religious Studies at the University of North Carolina at Chapel Hill, interested in questions about religion and governance, law, and the state. He hosts at the New Books Network Podcast and works as the Marketing and Communications Coordinator for both the North American Association for the Study of Religion (NAASR) and the American Academy of Religion Southeast region (AAR-SE).

Erica Bennett received her B.A. in Religious Studies at Millsaps College and her M.A. in Religious Studies from the University of Alabama. She spent much of her college career developing skills in research, museum studies, and podcasting/digital creation; she now works full-time as an Event Coordinator for the University of Alabama.

Pamela K. Gilbert is Albert Brick Professor in the Department of English at the University of Florida, working principally on nineteenth-century British literature, the history of the body and of medicine. Her books include *Victorian Skin: Surface, Self, History* (Cornell, 2019); *Disease, Desire and the Body in Victorian Women's Popular Novels* (Cambridge, 1997); *Mapping the Victorian Social Body* (SUNY, 2004), *The Citizen's Body* (Ohio State, 2007); and *Cholera and Nation* (SUNY, 2008).

Chapter 3

"What I'm Doing Is Pivoting My Career …": Life After Grad School with Jared Powell

Jacob Barrett, Erica Bennett, and Jared Powell

The following transcript is from the third episode of a four-part series on the University of Alabama's Study Religion podcast. The podcast was originally posted on September 6, 2022; it was hosted and produced by Erica Bennett while the transcript was produced by Erica and Jacob Barrett, now in his Ph.D. at the University of North Carolina at Chapel Hill. The guest is Jared Powell.

ERICA BENNETT: My name is Erica Bennett and I am a current student in the Religion *in* Culture Master's program at the University of Alabama. This is the third episode in a special series on the academic job market after graduate school in the humanities. In this episode, Jacob and I explore the experience of a student leaving a graduate program before completion. We listened to Jared Powell explain his decision to leave his Ph.D. program and what he plans to do next.

* * *

JARED POWELL: I did my undergraduate degree at the University of Alabama, where I was a double major in English and religious studies. I stuck around at Alabama for my first Master's in English, and then I started a Ph.D. program in English at the University of North Carolina at Chapel Hill. Just this past May, I decided to leave that program early, and so I've graduated with a second Master's in English from UNC.

ERICA BENNETT: Why did you first decide to go into a Ph.D. program?

JARED POWELL: I decided to go into a Ph.D. program because, for the longest time, I thought that I wanted to be a high school teacher. I decided I wanted to be a teacher back in high school, and then I went to undergrad and did the double major and really got into English, so I thought I would teach high school English. I have several cousins that are teachers and they said, "You should definitely get a Master's because you can get paid more." So, I went into my Master's still thinking I wanted to teach high school and was just doing it to get paid more. Over the course of the Master's, though, I really decided that the college levels were where I wanted to teach and that I wanted to be a professor because I really enjoyed the research that I did in my Master's.

I did plenty of research in undergrad as well, but it took on a whole different level in the Master's. So, that's when I decided to continue that and do the Ph.D. I went in fully wanting to be a professor, and I kind of always thought I would end up at a liberal arts college because I really enjoyed the research, but I really was always drawn more to the teaching. I went in wanting to be a professor and, as you guys know, to be a professor in most fields you have to do a Ph.D.

ERICA BENNETT: You just recently left your Ph.D. program. If you don't mind, could you explain that decision for us? What were the deciding factors in leaving your program?

JARED POWELL: There were many factors. It was many things kind of coming to head at once. I'll say first it started with the COVID-19 pandemic. The pandemic hit in Spring 2020, and that was my last semester of coursework. In English, we teach and that is how we get paid through our Ph.D. So, I was also teaching two classes that semester and, without going into too much detail, I can say that the pandemic took a huge toll on my mental health, and I found myself losing a lot of interest and drive in things like reading for my exams. I missed being in person. I missed seeing colleagues and just having casual conversations with them, and suddenly I was just stuck at home reading, grading, teaching. I love teaching, and I love my students, and really the students are what got me through the pandemic, but I did not enjoy teaching online for many of these reasons. I need that in-person contact to thrive, at least in the classroom setting.

Then, there was also seeing people who were a couple years ahead of me in the program who I thought were, quite frankly, much better job candidates than I am not even land a single first interview. That was really disheartening. I always had been told by so many people that the job market was terrible, but it was kind of just this vague future issue. People talked about it as a bridge to cross when I got there, and now suddenly, that bridge was fast approaching. That was really unnerving. I'd say those were probably the two main reasons. Then as well, seeing this kind of greater anti-higher education discourse in our current political moment was kind of disheartening for me.

One other thing to add is that it was hard to see how bleak the academic job market is, but I was also seeing my wife and my other friends who are not in this job market thriving. Outside of the academic job market over the pandemic, I saw people working from home, moving around, and getting higher raises. I was seeing friends thrive and thinking that maybe I wanted that.

ERICA BENNETT: So, we are in this pandemic and it is really hard. You are struggling, and then you realize that the academic job market is not what you are looking for. Knowing that you might need to get a job outside of the university system, what help did you receive from your program or your college or your university as a whole?

JARED POWELL: I'd say the assistance was kind of a mixed bag. I think there wasn't much official institutional assistance either from my department or from the college/university at any level. If it's out there, I didn't find it, and I looked. So, maybe there's something, but it's not easy to find. For instance, in my department we have a robust job support group that meets monthly for things about the academic job market like prepping C.V.s, prepping letters and statements. We don't have that for the non-academic job market. They occasionally brought in speakers, and that was very helpful. My department brought in a speaker from the business school at UNC to talk about some of these things like how we should start to market ourselves. That was great, but that sort of stuff only happened occasionally. It wasn't a regular thing. I can think of one instance where we had a panel of recent graduates from our program—one of whom was a professor and the other two were not—and that was great, but that was organized by the graduate student organization.

So as far as an institutional level of support, I didn't have much in that regard, and I don't think that that's unique to where I was. I did a Master's at a different institution, and it was the same way there. I'd say in my English department at Alabama there was not much institutional support, even for the majority of the M.A. students who were planning to be a high school teacher. I did have some great support on the individual level. All of my Ph.D. committee members happened to have all always been professors. There were some faculty members in my department that had done other careers, but they weren't on my committee. So when I told my committee my plans, they all said, "This is all we've ever done professionally, but we'll help you however we can. And we think this is the right decision." They were very helpful and very encouraging, connecting me with people that they knew or sending me job offers that they thought I might be a good fit for. A lot of the support was from individuals, but even then there was a limit to what they could do. Understandably, and I don't blame them because they have been in this career for a long time, so how can I expect them to really know what to do?

ERICA BENNETT: After hearing you say that and thinking back to what was said in another interview, it seems like there is a disconnect between the individual support from professors trying their best to help and the institution as a whole. Do you think there is a disconnect happening?

JARED POWELL: I agree. You know, I went to the career center, and I've sent students to the career center before, and I think it's wonderful for undergraduate students, but I didn't have a great experience as a graduate student going there. I went there to talk about how to turn my C.V. into a resume, and the person they paired me with was an undergraduate student intern who gave good advice, but not the advice I needed. It was the kind of advice that an undergraduate might need preparing their resume from scratch, but not a graduate student trying to pivot like I was doing. What I'm doing is pivoting my career, and there is all of this emphasis on that for the undergraduates. I noticed it at Alabama. I noticed it here at UNC. People said to the English majors that there were all of these things you could do with an English degree. For some reason, that just stopped once we get into graduate school. I guess the assumption is if you're in a Ph.D. program, you're going to be a professor, so that whole mentality that they do for undergrads just kind of doesn't happen.

ERICA BENNETT: I have seen that too, and that does make sense because of course you can do other things. We all have very marketable skills, but if you're going to tell me I can do everything with an English degree or that I can do so many things with a religious studies degree, you're going to have to help me see what those other things are. I may not know because I haven't experienced the job market before.

JARED POWELL: To get back to the point about the disconnect between the individual professors versus an institutional way of helping, I think the first step that has to happen is to recognize those individuals that are able to help. Like I said, we have some faculty members who have done other careers and come to academia. I think departments should be making committees with those faculty members and have them speak regularly to their graduate students. I'm sure they're already bringing them in to speak to their undergrads, but they need to bring them in to talk to their graduate students as well. I think that is the first place to start, perhaps.

ERICA BENNETT: What skills have you learned while in your Ph.D. program that are preparing you for the job market outside of academia? What skills do you think you have now?

JARED POWELL: Full disclosure that I am still looking for a job, so I can't say for sure what helped me get a job, but I can say what I hope will help me get a job. The Ph.D. gave me the ability to write well and to write in all sorts of different modes and genres. At least for the types of jobs I'm applying to, the ability to research is important and I'm really trying to bring those forward. I'm also trying to spin my teaching experience. I taught two classes a semester, and all of those interactions with students are interpersonal skills. I've got 19 students or 20 or however many students in a class who are all working on the same assignment, but each assignment has its own twist because it's their individual thing. So keeping track of that and who struggles with this and who excels at this and bringing all of those threads together to me demonstrates a set of skills that seem important to applications outside of academia. And working through a Ph.D. is project management. I like to think it is, and I'm trying to at least make that case in my job applications that it is project management experience in a way.

ERICA BENNETT: How did you come to see these experiences and skills as applicable outside of academia?

JARED POWELL: Some of these things I've come to on my own. With others, individual professors have put me in touch with people and those people have really helped. I've just been struck by how generous people have been with their time and giving advice. So, it's been a combination of reflecting on these skills and also talking to others who have been in a similar situation. One of my main contacts that's been very helpful has his Ph.D. in history from UNC and now works in digital product management at a bank. He has been very helpful in pointing to the skills that we have as academics that he used, whether they are ones I haven't thought of or he is confirming the ones I have thought of. So, I'd say it's a combination of self-reflection and advice from peers who have been through this.

ERICA BENNETT: You have a great point, though, that we can have great professors who are great humans and that it doesn't need to fall on their shoulders that we're trying to find these jobs.

JARED POWELL: I think it certainly doesn't need to fall on the graduate students' shoulders, though. We are underpaid and overworked. Every level of a university—the department level, the college level, the university as a whole—they keep track of their alumni and what the alumni are doing. It's time to pull on those networks. Sure, students can do that. They can hop on LinkedIn, and they can search whatever, but the institutions bear some of this responsibility and they should pull on these networks.

ERICA BENNETT: What would you say was the best advice and the worst advice you received while on your academic journey and now into your career journey?

JARED POWELL: Well, the best advice was advice I didn't follow. Looking back on it, though, it's the best advice. One of my undergraduate thesis advisors, and one of my absolute favorite professors at UA in English, asked me "Are you sure?" when I said I wanted to do a Ph.D. This was kind of my first taste of the "job market talk." He pushed me, and he said, "I think you should do law school. You should do something else. If there's anything else you can imagine yourself doing besides graduate school right now, I think you should try that first. Take a year or two and do something else. Then, if you still want to go back, go back." Of course, 21/22-year-old Jared was just like, "That's absurd. I know what I want to do. I'm not listening to you. How dare you." But, I wish I had listened to that advice. I think all the time that I needed a break and should have taken a break at some point between my undergraduate degree and graduate school to think about what else was out there that I could do and could be happy doing. So that was the best advice that I did not follow and now wish I had followed. And the worst advice, huh? I'd say there hasn't really been any bad advice, but there's been a lack of advice, you know?

ERICA BENNETT: Do you think if Ph.D. programs were set up differently and faculty were equipped to mentor students heading to all different career types that you would've needed the break to reconsider if you wanted to do graduate school?

JARED POWELL: I think a break from school still would've been nice just to have a break from school. That's something I tell all of my students no matter if they're considering graduate school at all. I don't quite get into the job market talk, but I do tell them that I wish I had taken that break. That is a good question though. If it wouldn't have been necessary in the same ways, if my program or my institution were set up to give this sort of assistance and help, I think a break probably still would've been nice, but it would've been more to prevent burnout and chill more than a time to explore other career options.

ERICA BENNETT: What do you think departments and institutions could do better to help their students moving forward?

JARED POWELL: I think drawing on those alumni networks. Like I said, in my department graduate students organized a panel of recent graduates—have that be a semesterly or at the least yearly event and have the department bringing these people in. Another thing is that graduate students don't get paid in the summer, so we seek out work in the summer and often it's in the form of internships. I did my first summer here at UNC on an internship. The reason I found out about it was because of a friend who was in the program a year before me did it. I told someone after me, and it's been a chain of English graduate students at UNC that have had that internship for like the past four years. I can think of other friends who have done other internships in the summer. If departments could find a way to give us credit hours for that, or some sort of degree certificate or something along those lines to recognize that that's work, I think that would be a good step.

Then, I think just being open to change is important. We think of academia as this liberal, free-thinking place to be, but I was involved in some student government last year and so I sat in on a lot of meetings and saw that things are slow to change. People at the university need to be listening to the needs of the graduate students and willing to adjust the curriculum or adjust practices in order to help students find jobs so that the needs are met.

ERICA BENNETT: What are your next steps? What jobs are you looking at? What do you think you're interested in now?

JARED POWELL: One hobby that I picked up over the pandemic was digital art, like 3D art, 3D modeling, pixel art, and a little bit of teaching myself some game development. That's the industry I'm trying to break into. That's my dream industry right now. I'm trying to break into the video game industry, ideally as a writer or a narrative designer or something like that where I can draw on that knowledge of literature and those research skills. I'm also looking more broadly at tech jobs.

ERICA BENNETT: Do you have any final thoughts?

JARED POWELL: I really liked the point about the disconnect between the individuals wanting to help and the institution laying the groundwork to do that help because my professors, my advisor, my committee have all been incredibly helpful and supportive these last six-seven months since I told them my plans. I am forever grateful for that. I just hope that they—not just UNC, not just UA, but departments everywhere in the humanities—can find a way to harness those individuals and make something. Institutions are made of individuals, and so the individuals with the mind to do this work are there. It is just a matter of bringing them together and giving them the resources they need so that it can become an institutional thing. I think it can be done. It's just going to take some work.

* * *

ERICA BENNETT: The interview with Jared really shows just how unprepared students are to leave the academy. We have acknowledged that the academic job market is hard to succeed in, but we are not preparing students to expand their job search. Jared explained that it is not a problem an individual can fix, but these are issues that go deep throughout the entire institution that the departments are a part of. The skills Jared has gained are extremely applicable to so many jobs outside academia, but he had to figure that out practically by himself with, of course, those closest to him offering all the help they could, but that still didn't seem like enough.

JACOB BARRETT: Jared really echoed some of the issues that Bradley Sommer experienced. So, to me, that shows that issues facing graduate students after graduation are systemic issues, not a sparse problem experienced within some humanities departments.

ERICA BENNETT: Do you think that people can thrive in non-academic jobs after a Ph.D. program?

JACOB BARRETT: Actually, that makes me think of Shannon Trosper Schorey. She got her Ph.D. from the University of North Carolina at Chapel Hill and is working outside of the academy right now.

Jacob Barrett is a Ph.D. student in the Department of Religious Studies at the University of North Carolina at Chapel Hill, interested in questions about religion and governance, law, and the state. He hosts at the New Books Network Podcast and works as the Marketing and Communications Coordinator for both the North American Association for the Study of Religion (NAASR) and the American Academy of Religion Southeast region (AAR-SE).

Erica Bennett received her B.A. in Religious Studies at Millsaps College and her M.A. in Religious Studies from the University of Alabama. She spent much of her college career developing skills in research, museum studies, and podcasting/digital creation; she now works full-time as an Event Coordinator for the University of Alabama.

Jared Powell earned a B.A. in English and Religious Studies and then an M.A. in English at the University of Alabama and then began a Ph.D. in English at UNC Chapel Hill, specializing in the poetry of William Blake. After much deliberation, he decided to leave his program to pivot to a career outside of the academy. He now works as a trainer for a software company, putting his teaching and curriculum design experience to good use.

Chapter 4

"Be Thoughtful About What Skills You're Developing …": Life After Grad School with Shannon Trosper Schorey

Jacob Barrett, Erica Bennett, and Shannon Trosper Schorey

The following transcript is from the last episode of a four-part series on the University of Alabama's Study Religion podcast. The podcast was originally posted on September 6, 2022; it was hosted and produced by Erica Bennett while the transcript was produced by Erica and Jacob Barrett, now in his Ph.D. at the University of North Carolina at Chapel Hill. The guest is Shannon Trosper Schorey.

ERICA BENNETT: My name is Erica Bennett, and I am a current student in the Religion *in* Culture Master's program at the University of Alabama. This is the fourth and final episode in a special series on the academic job market after graduate school in the humanities. In this episode, Jacob and I learn about a non-academic career path after a Ph.D. program as Shannon Trosper Schorey tells us about her experience leaving academia and entering the tech industry.

* * *

SHANNON TROSPER SCHOREY: I completed my Ph.D. in religious studies from the University of North Carolina at Chapel Hill in 2018, where I explored the intersection of religious history and technology. I work at Red Hat, a software company. The questions I pursued at UNC included, "How are technological communities thinking about technology, explaining technology, and explaining to each other how technology works? How are those ideas still invested in religious language and Protestant assumptions about the world?" That led me to write a chapter on open source, a particular way of writing and sharing software that has an ideological commitment to open access and modification. Red Hat is one of the major open-source companies so it was on my radar.

I received a fellowship in 2017 that allowed me to just write for the year, which was the dream—but I ended up feeling isolated. I was writing and spinning my wheels and looking at the academic job market—seeing how few jobs there were and how a lot of them were short term positions. At that point, I had already uprooted my husband twice. He had a wonderful job at our undergrad that he gave up when we moved to Boulder. He did it again three years later for Chapel Hill. I decided I would only ask him to pause his career again for something truly important and meaningful to me. I wanted to be a good partner because he'd been such a good partner.

So, this job at Red Hat popped up and I thought, "You know what? I'll apply. I think I fit 70–80% of the job description," which I've had people tell me all my life that's all you need to apply to something. There was nothing riding on the application since I was just writing for the year, it didn't really matter if I got it or not, but I thought it could be interesting field work if I did. I got the job. I now work as a principal communications specialist, which means I do a lot of writing, editing, interviewing stakeholders, literature reviews, analyst research, and content strategy. It's not so different from work I did with students—I help smart folks think through the information we've collected and find a way to say something interesting and evidenced about it.

ERICA BENNETT: When you started your Ph.D., was this even on your radar of jobs and, if not, what were you first planning to pursue after your Ph.D.?

SHANNON TROSPER SCHOREY: Not at all. Tech was on my research radar because I knew that I wanted to think about how delightfully weird discourses about tech can get, it had always resonated with me as an interesting area to think about secularism and religion. Working in tech, though, was not at all on my radar.

I was pretty narrow-minded when I thought about my career. I was focused on making sure I had the raw materials ready for an academic job. I published early and relatively often. I did the international and the national conference circuit. I taught. I did the Graduate Studies Committee stuff. I didn't know how to think about alternatives. I think what led me to the alternative was being at that specific moment in my marriage and life, looking at the job market, knowing that tenure track jobs were rare and that a postdoc or visiting position likely meant not just one or two years of moving, but up to 10 years of it. I was watching talented friends who were in these positions and dealing with the market in real time. So, I just got curious and a little whimsical. I applied to Red Hat without thinking too much about it. I was still a year out from applying to academic jobs, so it was a good time to apply because it was a little like buying a lottery ticket for something else.

ERICA BENNETT: How did you stumble across this job at Red Hat?

SHANNON TROSPER SCHOREY: It was a combination of being familiar with open source and Red Hat, Red Hat being in Raleigh, and deciding a few years earlier that I wanted some networks that were not other graduate students. I reached a point in my third year where all my social networks were graduate students. I loved my peers, but it was too easy to talk about work all the time. So I started going to a meetup about watching horror movies. We would show up at a random house in Chapel Hill and watch horror movies with 20 other people from around the triangle. One of those people worked at Red Hat. She posted the job on social media and I reached out to her and said, "Okay, you know what? It sounds like a writing job. Tell me about it."

ERICA BENNETT: Now that also sounds like a potential horror movie!

SHANNON TROSPER SCHOREY: It does, but see, I love horror movies. In general, I think going to watch horror movies at an unknown person's house that you found on the internet is a risky endeavor, but it was truly wonderful.

ERICA BENNETT: So partly it sounds like a lot of luck. I think that's similar within the academic job market and outside the academic job market. There's always this portion of luck. Are you going to get there at the right time? Are you going to get the job you want? Or are you going to just hear about it through someone you might know?

SHANNON TROSPER SCHOREY: It's important to highlight luck, because I think a lot of what prevents people from looking for other jobs is an implicit belief in meritocracy within the academic system. So, if you do all the things and you do them well and you work all the time, you will get the tenure track job because the people that get it do so because of their ability—and it's true! Those are talented people who deserve those jobs. But there are lots more talented people who don't, and this belief in meritocracy ignores networks and luck.

I used to think networking was a gross term, and it can be, like, "I'm going to network with you to use you." But networking can also be as simple as just being radically interested in other people and lifting them up when you can. "Networking" got a lot better for me when I took the goal out of it. If I'm telling myself the goal is to get people interested in me, my social anxiety is stupid and I feel gross. But finding and uplifting community makes you a part of something.

When I started at UNC Chapel Hill there was a cohort that modeled this. They were generous, collaborative, and had made a pact to lift each other up and put each other in conversation with folks that they knew that each other didn't know. That made such a big difference in my life, having that model of professionalism. It gave me a way to approach networking with the language of "What are you interested in? Tell me about your work. What makes you excited?"

ERICA BENNETT: Is there anything that you wish was different about the academic system in the sense of what skills you wish you might have gained through your multiple years in academia?

SHANNON TROSPER SCHOREY: That's a great question. In terms of skills, the Ph.D. gave me almost everything. What it didn't give me was the ability to translate those skills to other people.

The skillset you build when you're in a graduate program includes close reading, the ability to ask cutting questions, to understand that any issue has several different layers of interpretation, the knowledge that those layers are going to be uneven because of history, power, and location, and the ability to start to pick apart that complexity and not be overwhelmed by it.

For example, project management is a thing people get paid well for and every single grad student I've ever met is a project manager who is unafraid of messy processes, can take an impossible task—like writing a thesis or doing a dissertation or creating a podcast series—and break it up into milestones and deliverables, define and track metrics, show success and show progress. Everybody's self-starting and knows how to collaborate, even with personal tensions and hierarchical dynamics. These are skills that are hard to gain in other contexts and are extremely valuable in other industries.

One of the problems is that Ph.D. programs don't tell you to focus on those things. They teach us that we are an expert in a specific area of research, and that the subject of the research is the crucial part. I have a friend, also a Ph.D. in religious studies, who pointed this out to me. She's a User Experience (UX) researcher at Microsoft. I told her I was hesitant to apply to UX positions because of lack of experience. She was like, "You absolutely have UX research skills, why is your dissertation just listed here as a dissertation? You were a principal researcher for a multi-year project that you designed, managed, wrote, and funded with grant money." Those are the things we need to translate, what we're actually doing when we get a Ph.D., or organize a conference, or teach, etc.

ERICA BENNETT: It's not that you don't gain the skills in your academic journey. It's that you lose the skills of how to explain them to people outside of your academic community. So, to anyone in academia, if I say I did a dissertation, they think of all those things. "Oh wow. She, she did this project for multiple years. Oh my gosh. She also got a grant." They hear those words as soon as they hear "dissertation." Outside of our little bubble, though, no one quite knows exactly what that entails because they've not done one. They want to know how doing a dissertation can benefit them and their company. It makes sense that the skill you need is knowing how to translate this to people outside of academia.

SHANNON TROSPER SCHOREY: Which you also have if you do any teaching! This is a big part of my work at Red Hat too. Experts talking to experts is this wonderfully productive space in which they can communicate so many things with one word, but they lose anybody not already in the room if they don't slow it down. Academics are the same way.

ERICA BENNETT: Do you often have graduate students come and ask you questions about the job market outside of academia? How do you advise them?

SHANNON TROSPER SCHOREY: I do. I think everyone who I've talked to who has left academia has people sliding into their emails. It is kind of an underground network because it's a harsh moment—if you finish the Ph.D., you are maybe 10 years into graduate school. That is a serious investment of time and resources. Often it's delayed financial planning, delayed family planning, moving to places where they may or may not feel comfortable or safe. It's a lot to invest with a very small goal post of success, because the goal post that's celebrated is not getting the Ph.D. but getting a tenure-track job. The internet tells me that something like 3% of the world's population has a Ph.D. But we're not going to celebrate that—you only count if you get a tenure track job. Or, you only count if you are at this or that institution. With so much invested, thinking about alternatives can feel like a dream dying. If you leave now, what did you do it all for? If you stay, what are the chances you get to that goal? Not to mention, who are you if you aren't an academic?

I think it's a conversation that is getting louder, even over the past year, but I don't think it can happen fully until that issue is addressed.

ERICA BENNETT: Right! Who is going to pop the bubble? Who is going to pop the dream bubble that everyone who gets a Ph.D. is going to be a professor one day? No one wants to pop that bubble because I think as soon as you do, now you're worried if anyone is even going to want a Ph.D. So who inside the Ph.D. system wants to pop that bubble when that means they don't have anyone wanting to get a Ph.D.?

SHANNON TROSPER SCHOREY: I'm so glad you phrased it this way because this kills me. Higher education is being defunded, the public at large is swinging into an anti-intellectual space. Academics are part of a very threatened thing. So of course, part of what anyone does when they are threatened, is say, "Well, we are special. You need us." But then it has a tendency to collapse into the same sort of language we were talking about before: "We are special because the research is special and you can't do this outside of academia." Which even if true doesn't reach an audience who isn't already invested in that subject being important on its own. I want to make it clear that I'm not arguing that the only way or best way to defend higher ed is through a business case and crass logic, but the flip side is that graduate students are inside of a system that is telling them that they are special because of one specific thing and that, even if they have the skills to leave the institution, if they leave they are failing.

ERICA BENNETT: They are told that they didn't have the stamina to stay at seven adjunct professorships for a hundred years with your two kids and jump between seven states. How dare you leave your goal of being a professor!

SHANNON TROSPER SCHOREY: And after the first year of adjuncting it becomes even harder to get the tenure-track job! So you have folks who are in a system where they can't imagine alternatives (or are told not to) and then this becomes the only meaningful career path to them because they have invested everything to do this. I think for a lot of people there is a moment of real grief and grappling with what to do and who you are when you can't, or decide not to, work in academia.

One of the things that I tell people who do ask me if I am glad I went to a Ph.D. program is that I am so glad I went. I am so glad I got the Ph.D. because I am a fundamentally different person because of UNC Chapel Hill. I am a different thinker. I have a different perspective than many of my coworkers and friends. The way I engage with the world is different. Having that time where a significant part of your job is to read and engage in conversations that have been going on across time and geography is such a gift. Until we talk about why it's a beautiful thing, distinct from the tenure-track, we are in a losing position to defend higher education.

ERICA BENNETT: The goal doesn't need to be a tenure-track professorship. The goal could be gaining knowledge. The goal could be a tech job, or the goal could be X, Y, and Z. I think that's really interesting to put it that way, that the goal doesn't have to be this tenure-track position.

SHANNON TROSPER SCHOREY: Well, it's also an interesting thing to talk about goals. A friend at Red Hat pointed out to me that academics have an almost treadmill-like understanding of career development, they are used to a formalized path that says "You do this and this and this." Other careers don't work that way and you don't commit to a job for a lifetime. So, when he looks for a different position, his goals are even phrased differently than anything that I was formulating. He made me really stop and rethink what "the goal of the Ph.D." was for me, and if that was even the right language? Could the goal of a Ph.D., or even the "business case" for higher education, be a voting public that can discriminate against falsified information or ask sharper questions or champion inclusivity and diverse voices in ways that are held to a higher standard?

But we only have the space to reimagine goals and make these arguments if graduate students are paid a living wage. As long as there are still students taking out loans, then the "why" relies on the promise of a job.

ERICA BENNETT: How would you advise someone still in their Ph.D. program who realizes that they want to go outside the academic field? What things should they be thinking about? What should they be looking for? How should they be communicating their skills that we know they have?

SHANNON TROSPER SCHOREY: The first thing I would say is do not take out loans for a graduate program. In the best-case scenario you're going to have graduate school paid for, and that is the only scenario you should go with. Even then, it is a pause on your retirement and your savings, and that pause is really felt when you are on the job market and it adds a layer of pressure and grief. If you're looking at graduate school, you have other options. Take care of your financial life first and only go somewhere where you are valued and supported with a living wage.

The second thing I would say is to be curious and be open and look at your training as a job. Be thoughtful about what skills you're developing and practice translating those for yourself. Keep track of the things you do and look for related job postings, see how they are describing the same skills and start walking yourself through how that translates. And then, if you find a piece of some project that you really like, like teaching or research, look at similar jobs and figure out what else they require. I have a friend from UNC who is now a project manager, he loved that part of the process. After graduating he got the Project Management Professional (PMP) certification and that, combined with his grad experience, allowed him to enter a mid-level job.

So, I think being open, being curious, knowing the value of what you're doing and the good that it's giving to you for the time that you're in the Ph.D. program is important. You have the five to seven years, or the two to three years in the master's program, and it is important to treasure that for what it is, but also not to get caught in the imagination of your committee. These are people who have succeeded within the system. They're brilliant people, but maybe also, they're not the ones who are best equipped to help you think about what else you can do. So, start meeting people—talking to alumni, joining a horror meetup, or literally anything else.

Think about it as though you are in control of your career. Even if you want the tenure-track job, you don't have to be on that treadmill. I think it is very easy to get into a Ph.D. program and get really overwhelmed by everything you need to accomplish. You are handed a packet that is like, "By year three, you're going to do languages and by three and a half, you're going to do exams. By year four, you're going to do your prospectus, year five you're going to write," and it is all laid out. I think you have to say, "Okay, this is what I need to do. But also, how do I want to set my own professional development goals? What do I want or need out of this experience?"

ERICA BENNETT: Also, I just thought of this but language knowledge has to be a great, marketable skill. I always forget that a lot of Ph.D. programs have you do languages.

SHANNON TROSPER SCHOREY: It is! I have a friend who is constantly looking at the Pokémon company because they know Japanese. I know somebody else finishing her Ph.D. who is a freelancer translating board games, it sounds like so much fun!

ERICA BENNETT: There are so many options. We've talked about what individual students can be doing. Do you think there is anything that institutions, especially departments in the humanities, could implement to better prepare their students leaving their programs?

SHANNON TROSPER SCHOREY: That's a great question. The first thing is pay graduate students, full stop. It's a job. It's a job and there's that horrible issue where graduate students are differently classified as student or staff and it affects insurance, leave, etc. If you pay students so that they can live while doing a program and not leave with debt and loans, that solves a lot of issues. It allows people to make a choice to go do this for other professional development reasons outside of the academic job market. I chose to go do it, to learn how to be a thinker and rapidly gain professionalization skills that are hugely benefiting me in the corporate world. That's just the reality. When you switch a career, you have to be ready to enter a more junior position, but in every case I've seen with Ph.D.s, even if they start out more junior, they rapidly get promoted to senior mid-level positions and catch up to their peers who have been doing the job the whole time—and that's because they have skills that are hard to teach. But, it has to start with departments and universities paying graduate students and not offering positions if they can't pay for them fully.

Departments can and should create alumni networks. Faculty are pressed with time and are suffering under the same system. Rather than them having to shoulder all the weight of preparing students to leave a system that they are still deeply invested in, alumni can help. If you have a robust alumni network, what you're also doing is showing your grad students all sorts of versions of success. You are showing that they are still part of this intellectual community even if they go do something else. Diverse alumni will also demonstrate all the different things that could be possible after the program, opening up the imagination of everything students could do without relying on tired and vague marketing.

Identifying complimentary skills is also important. We've all been in the C.V. workshops but what about resumes? Departments should encourage students to be looking at job descriptions and thinking about how to tailor their Ph.D. experience to those sorts of skills. Is there a way to incorporate related job skills (like analytics, design, or SEO) into that student's research plan? Maybe it doesn't make sense for everybody to do a dissertation. Public portfolios are really important. Departments can start thinking about what students can produce if they are a talented humanities researcher. You want to go into videography? Can you produce a documentary in the archives? Departments need to think about how students can be academically rigorous but still produce something that you can hand over in an interview. There's a system for letters of recommendation in place for academic jobs. Faculty need to learn how to write letters and little blurbs that can help students in different contexts. So, maybe it's opening part of the letter for the student to use, or maybe it's adding something to their LinkedIn, or writing a testimonial for their freelance website. There's a wealth of ideas, departments just need to start trying some stuff.

ERICA BENNETT: Talking to you today has been really nice and refreshing because we're not trying to beat down the academic system by any means. That's not the goal of this podcast. We all know we're in the same bus and we're all struggling with the same fight. We talked to Pamela Gilbreth, who is a professor at the University of Florida, who said when she was going on the job market she was struggling with the same problems in the nineties. So, we need to be acknowledging that this isn't a new problem and acknowledging that there are steps that programs can be doing to help. We talked to a lot of people who had problems with their college career centers with them not even being able to help a graduate student try to find a job outside of their track. So, talking to you has been really refreshing because it's not this like, "No one has hope." It's like, "We all think education is important, but now let's see how more important it can be than just being a professor." Being a professor is great, but that is not the argument. We must acknowledge that there is a problem.

SHANNON TROSPER SCHOREY: I think it's a "we should all be friends" argument. People need to be financially supported and stable to be able to do anything— that has to be addressed first. Then, we need to be recognizing that graduate students are the most vulnerable, but there's pressure all the way up the system, and all the way up the system, the language being used to defend higher education is failing. So how can we take the pressure off of the people who are the most vulnerable, while also starting to think about why we are doing any of this beyond job placement. Higher education is a beautiful and amazing thing and the world will be extremely worse off if we lose it.

* * *

ERICA BENNETT: I loved talking with Shannon because she not only gave advice for students who are adventuring outside of academia, but she gave specific examples of different things departments and institutions can implement to aid their students entering those job.

JACOB BARRETT: Totally. I think her advice for Ph.D. students finding new language to talk about the skills that they have, whether it's our project management skills or other kinds of skills that non-academic jobs are looking for that Ph.D. students have and are equipped for but just talk about differently. I thought that was really interesting. I also like what she had to say about how departments should be utilizing their alumni that have jobs outside of the academy as resources. When the faculty don't know how to answer a question, those alumni who were successful in their graduate programs and got their Ph.D. and are now successful in a field outside of academia can serve as a resource to those students as well.

ERICA BENNETT: So, listening to all these interviews was a lot of information. Do you feel better about going into your Ph.D. program or are you more nervous and, with that, what do you think was one of your biggest takeaways?

JACOB BARRETT: I definitely feel better. I think it's one of those things where I now know more in depth people's experiences, and know a little more about the problem as well as having lots of really useful tips and advice on how to navigate this. As I work my way through the Ph.D. program, and if at some point I decide that I want to pursue a career outside of academia, it is good to know I have been working with those skills in the back of my head so that I can make that pivot at any moment and be successful, whether I decide to pursue academia or pivot and pursue a non-academic job.

ERICA BENNETT: I found these interviews super helpful in understanding that it's not a specific department's problem. It's not a specific field's problem. It's truly the humanities as a whole and possibly more than just the humanities. We have talked to a history Ph.D., an English professor, a former English Ph.D. student, and a religious studies Ph.D. We have truly run the gambit of departments from universities across multiple states to show that we're in this together, and that it's not just an isolated issue at one liberal arts college down the road. It is felt at big state schools, small liberal arts colleges, and everything in between. So, we have to prepare not only our students for leaving our programs, but we also have to prepare our faculty that are already in the systems because without all of us understanding that this is a larger problem than just ourselves, none of us will be able to help each other.

JACOB BARRETT: Thank you so much, Erica. This has been so helpful and I feel a lot better about starting my Ph.D. program. I always love chatting, but I'm actually running late for orientation, so I have to hop off and head over there. Talk soon!

* * *

ERICA BENNETT: Thank you so much for listening to this series. We are very grateful to have had so many people willing to participate and educate not only those going into a graduate program, but also those already in the academy. Graduates from programs of all shapes and sizes are struggling. We created this series to shine a small light on a problem that requires the attention and action of all of those who are proud to be in academia. Education is valuable. Do not let these issues continue to be pushed under the rug until students no longer want to enroll in higher education. College is a time to learn, explore, and prepare for a life after school. Let's help our students do that at all levels, and for all potential careers.

Jacob Barrett is a Ph.D. student in the Department of Religious Studies at the University of North Carolina at Chapel Hill, interested in questions about religion and governance, law, and the state. He hosts at the New Books Network Podcast and works as the Marketing and Communications Coordinator for both the North American Association for the Study of Religion (NAASR) and the American Academy of Religion Southeast region (AAR-SE).

Erica Bennett received her B.A. in Religious Studies at Millsaps College and her M.A. in Religious Studies from the University of Alabama. She spent much of her college career developing skills in research, museum studies, and podcasting/digital creation; she now works full-time as an Event Coordinator for the University of Alabama.

Shannon Trosper Schorey, who earned her Ph.D. at the University of North Carolina, Chapel Hill, is a Principal Communications Specialist in the tech industry as well as a freelance writer and editor of fiction and nonfiction. Her work has appeared in *The Dread Machine*, *Punk Noir Magazine*, *Machines in Between*, and *Religion Dispatches*.

Manifesto

Chapter 5

A Manifesto on Earning and Awarding a Ph.D.

Andrew Ali Aghapour, Shannon Trosper Schorey,
Thomas J. Whitley, Vaia Touna, and Russell T. McCutcheon

Relying on the collaborative input from doctoral graduates in the study of religion who have gone on to successful careers outside of academia, this chapter offers a critique of the field for not adapting far quicker to the changing economic conditions of higher education over recent decades but also provides a variety of practical suggestions for how programs in our field can make tactical and substantive changes to better prepare graduate students for a far wider variety of professional futures, inasmuch as we all know that few, at least for the foreseeable future, will ever be hired as tenure-track faculty members.

On Saturday, March 12, 2022, the second remote panel of the annual Method & Theory in the Study of Religion section at the southeast regional conference of the American Academy of Religion featured an open discussion with Andrew Ali Aghapour, Shannon Trosper Schorey, and Thomas J. Whitley. As described in the conference program, "[t]his panel and discussion focus on the relevance of the skills gained in Religious Studies classes—skills that prepare students for a wider variety of futures than may not at first be apparent to both them and their professors. The panelists—all holding recent Ph.D.s in the study of religion—will discuss their experience creating successful professional futures for themselves, with an eye toward making practical recommendations that Departments of Religious Studies can adopt to better serve their B.A., M.A., and Ph.D. students." Because so few people sometimes attend such sessions, despite the fact that, at least in this case, the issues being addressed impact *the entire profession*, the panelists and organizers decided that the message of the panel was well worth amplifying by collaborating on a follow-up publication.[1] What follows, then, is both a brief rationale for such a manifesto and a series of practical recommendations aimed at various members of the field. Some of these recommendations can be easily implemented or have an immediate effect while others require long term dedication, careful monitoring, and the commitment of continuing resources. Our proposals are designed to help students, faculty, and administrators address longstanding trends in the humanities that, in our estimation, greatly constrain the field, both now and for the foreseeable future. For instance, earning the highest research degree in the humanities continues, for the most part, to be conceived as a way of credentialing those seeking employment as a tenure-track faculty member, but this is an assumption that we find to be far too limiting given worrisome trends in higher ed; it overlooks the many other benefits that holding such a graduate degree in the humanities can offer, if only we were all more intentional and entrepreneurial about training graduate students.

Concerning the recommendations that follow: while these may be read as mere suggestions or perhaps strong guidance, they are in fact intended as necessary directives and even imperatives—thus our characterization of this document as a manifesto: a public declaration of something more than evident to the authors; for, in our estimation, the time is now long past when graduate programs in the field might merely consider implementing such proposals. Instead, continuing on well-trod curricular paths without reassessing the overall *purpose* and then also the *process* of earning a humanities research degree in the early twenty-first century strikes the authors as irresponsible and reckless. Especially, if we consider the accumulated debt on the part of students and, as will be described below, the various stressors that have adversely impacted academia's job market over past decades. The intention behind this document is therefore to start a national conversation between students and faculty, spanning departments and perhaps even national boundaries, to the benefit of the entire field.

But with the study of religion specifically in mind, our hope is also to inspire members of the field to reconsider how they carry out their work and thereby train their students. Starting with the suggestion that religion and any of its sub-components (i.e., those things commonly known as religious traditions, myths, rituals, texts, organizations, etc.), is no longer seen as uniquely meaningful, we would argue that the non-field specific methods necessary for novel and interesting work in our field (e.g., description, comparison, analysis, etc.) can also be applied in innumerable career settings, most of which are distant from both the university and what the study of religion has long been assumed to be about. For despite the days of seeing the culmination of our training to lie in pastoral or divinity training being long behind us, assumptions about religion's special nature remain prominent enough that few in our field seem able to think creatively about how our degree programs can be reconfigured in such trying times, to ensure not only that all of our students can find satisfying careers for themselves but that the field continues to offer classes and degree programs to interested students and to find a new relevance beyond the academy. Our hope, in writing this manifesto, is to help lead the field in just that direction.

Preamble

The challenges now facing newly minted Ph.Ds. in the humanities who are seeking full-time, let alone tenure-track, employment in academia are profoundly obvious to anyone with even just a passing familiarity with disillusioned academics posting sobering anecdotes about the current job market to various social media sites. What is sometimes not as evident, however, is that this is a challenge for the future of the entire field, if not the profession of being a university professor itself, rather than something that is simply isolated to a delimited set of individuals who now happen to have the unfortunate task of looking for work in academia; to rephrase, individualizing what in our estimation is a structural issue is a misrecognition that will only perpetuate the problem, as if having just one more peer review article listed on a C.V. would have made an applicant a contender. But sadly, this is precisely what has happened over the preceding few decades; for the bottom began falling out of viable academic careers in the humanities long before many who are now confronting its challenges were born and, again in our estimation, little has so far been done in our field to address it *in a systematic and effective manner.*

Now, in observing the longevity of the problem it certainly must be noted that the extent to which the so-called academic jobs crisis has increased since, for example, the 2008 worldwide financial collapse, let alone in the wake of COVID-19 protocols' more recent and sometimes dire effects on government budgets and thus university funding (what some now refer to as the COVID recession), has heightened the problem dramatically.[2] However, despite what undoubtedly now feels to some as a change in kind and not just extent, the longstanding nature of this problem means that virtually no one now working in academia can plead ignorance to the challenges currently facing those who are hoping to become full-time members of the field.[3] For we cannot forget that those faculty who have just reached, or are nearing, retirement came of age as young scholars in the mid- to late 1980s, when the once hoped-for retirement of the academic generation that had hastily been hired to teach the waves of post-World War II baby boomers (who began entering the university from the mid-1960s onward) failed to materialize, thereby giving the lie to the late 1980s and early 1990s tales of plentiful academic jobs to come. Unfortunately, what did come during this period was a steady decline in government budgets[4] and changing university priorities. Administrators during this period made the rational (at least in economic terms) decision to reduce instructional costs by staffing much of the university with far less expensive limited term full-time, part-time, and adjunct teachers, or those now collectively known as contingent faculty (i.e., the variety of faculty whose appointments are not on the tenure-track).[5] It is therefore almost impossible to imagine many who are now working in academia as being oblivious to this trend, one that has disproportionately impacted those academic disciplines often grouped together as the humanities, in distinction from the so-called social sciences as well as the disciplines that comprise the natural sciences.[6] As a result of decades of cuts and reallocations of resources the smooth career path once assumed to govern the lives of students entering the field (i.e., earning a B.A. then an M.A., entering a Ph.D and within four to 5 years applying for and gaining employment in a tenure-track faculty line) ceased to be a credible presumption some time ago. In fact, it has become increasingly common for many who have earned the highest degree in the field to have little choice but to work in perpetually insecure contingent positions in academia, sometimes simultaneously at multiple colleges, or (again, exercising a rational choice of their own) to leave the university entirely for what are, by and large, self-invented positions in other sectors of the economy (sometimes referred to as alt-ac careers)[7]—positions and thus careers almost completely unanticipated by (and therefore usually uncelebrated by) their doctoral programs. The pressures requiring our doctoral students to shift their career plans have by now made this "alternate" career path the norm in many cases, which makes our field's lack of collective action to address it all the more damning.

This means that, notably in the humanities and especially in the study of religion, faculty who long ago gained the seniority necessary to now administer departments, along with their undergraduate and graduate programs, cannot plead that any of this is news to them. But, as already suggested, there has been little, if any, structural changes in the way that our profession trains its graduate students and our reason for doing so. To phrase it another way, providing teaching experience, implementing C.V. writing workshops, mentoring cover-letter writing, or instituting mock academic job interviews—innovations that are now pretty routine in some, but not all, of our field's graduate programs—are, despite the fanfare which sometimes accompanies them, entirely inadequate developments that function as responses to problems facing the field decades ago. They are insufficient today because they fail to address the realities facing early career scholars who have *few if any* academic jobs to which they can even apply. This makes it all the more troubling to realize that, despite a very few notable exemptions, the M.A. degree's curriculum and requirements are still generally seen as preparatory for applying to a doctoral program and the curriculum and requirements for the doctorate still largely presume eventual work as an advanced researcher employed as a faculty member.[8] For a variety of reasons—such as the many current faculty members who have succumbed to the career's many inducements and perks—there has been little thinking outside of the box when it comes to redesigning both undergraduate and graduate curricula from the ground up, along with rethinking the rationale for earning our field's highest research degree, in the context of a radically changed economy and thus university. For, as already suggested, despite the manner in which society of the late twentieth and early twenty-first centuries has changed—like it or not—graduate education in our field still functions much as it has for over one hundred years, i.e., identifying an ever more focused and therefore arcane research specialty and investigating it for an extended period of time, for the benefit of an invariably small group of like-interested specialists. But how the definitional, descriptive, comparative, interpretive, and explanatory skills regularly taught and used in our programs might impact fields that have little to do with the data of the religious studies classroom (what some recently named as applied religious studies) has been largely unexplored.[9]

While faculty inaction in these trying circumstances has, in our view, certainly contributed to the problems now facing early career scholars—anecdotes of graduate students still arriving on the job market with little to no preparation from their doctoral advisors are too numerous to mention here, as are the doctoral supervisors who apparently continue to see anything occupying a grad student's time (e.g., publishing peer review essays, writing books reviews, networking and presenting at conferences, gaining teaching experience, etc.) as an unworthy distraction from writing a so-called "field changing dissertation"—we would be remiss not to acknowledge that current faculty members are themselves often working in undesirable situations of their own, *created by the very same factors that have so constrained the job market in recent decades*: from ever-increasing teaching and service expectations placed upon them to escalating expectations from administrators for more annual research, publishing, and citation productivity. It therefore seems unlikely that many of these faculty—people understandably intent to put their own traditional training to good use in largely traditional graduate programs—see any incentive to posing some of the tough questions about why someone might wish to earn a graduate degree in the study of religion, despite the fact that the onetime linkage between that credential and secure and rewarding full-time work in higher education has turned out to be more mythic than actual.[10] Instead, their time is likely best used, or so they may reason, in devising ways to lighten their own teaching duties so as to publish more, something still seen by many as their ticket toward their individual career progress. That their own continued relevance and even the future of their departments (thereby impacting their own future employment as faculty) might be linked to finally posing difficult structural questions about graduate education, and entertaining how to rethink their degree programs and even departments as a whole, may therefore be lost on them, what with their short term focus and creative energy so often devoted mostly to the many daily tasks that frequently accompany faculty in the modern university.[11] But even those faculty who may make honest efforts towards such changes often have little choice but to do so on an individual level, with their creative endeavors sometimes running against obstacles which are beyond their control—from the inertia of colleagues and departments to the expectations of university administrators and credentialing associations.

And so it is with all of this in mind that we return to the 2022 regional AAR session that bore the name of this paper's main title, as well as the following succinct list of directives from those who are best placed to offer them, i.e., recent alums of U.S. doctoral programs who, thanks to their own creativity, energy, and networking, are succeeding elsewhere but who retain enough affinity with the programs that trained them as scholars to prompt them each to reach back to assist us all to move forward in novel and effective ways. The goal, then, is to help stimulate students and faculty (i) to recognize, without illusions, the actual conditions in which they today work and (ii) to organize around a series of practical, if incremental, changes that can have a consequential effect—changes that may involve reconsidering the reasons for embarking on graduate education in the field, what one does during such training, and what can be done with such degrees after graduation. So, the key is to rethink M.A. and Ph.D. programs in the humanities based on the changes and demands of our current state of affairs, amplifying to the extent possible not just the content of our work but also the many skills that we all know a degree in the humanities can offer; we need to be more intentional about conveying those skills and integrating their applicability into the structure of graduate programs.

While we do not delude ourselves into thinking that any such list of suggestions will ever be definitive or even constructive in all settings, coming as the following list largely does from a group of doctoral graduates who have success-fully built diverse careers for themselves outside of academia—often despite a lack of mentoring toward such an end—we have confidence that those entering or already enrolled in graduate programs as well as those who are contribut-ing to and administering them will benefit from the hard won experience that animates each of these suggestions (which are organized around their intended audience). And should, as we hope, this list as a whole, and the rationale that drives it, prompt larger and ongoing conversations across the field, concerning how the study of religion can survive or perhaps even thrive in higher ed's cur-rent conditions, then all the better. For while it may appear as mere semantics to some, framing our present setting as a crisis, as we at times have done in the above, may itself be part of the problem.[12] Perhaps it is instead an opportunity to do something entirely new with the sometimes taken-for-granted or even over-looked, unrecognized and unrewarded skills that we've all along been learning in our classes, teaching to our students, and relying upon in our work.

Theses

Generalities

1. If the medium is the message, then in an ever-increasing digital and market-based world our traditional humanities message is becoming increasingly irrelevant.

2. We therefore have to make the change that we want to see become part of the system. That is, change at a single department or program-level is not sufficient. Changes must be scalable and widely applied and so we need to institutionalize our reimagining of the humanities doctoral degree among deans, provosts, presidents, state university systems, professional associations, and conferences, let alone among the general public, government, and the so-called private sector.

3. It is up to us to explain to a variety of constituencies why what we do matters and to do so in ways that those outside our field in particular and academia in general can understand. Therefore, universities, graduate schools, departments, and programs must invest time, money, and bureaucratic goodwill into modeling and fostering high quality public scholarship that is integrated into the heart of graduate training. This means preparing faculty and graduate students to effectively communicate to the broader public through the media and proactively working to connect media outlets with relevant researchers.

4. Just as nothing must be taught,[13] no tradition associated with graduate education must be continued; this applies chiefly to producing the monograph-length dissertation as a culminating

work. It is long past time for terminal research projects that mix media, outputs, and intended audiences. For the once standard focus on writing seminar papers, comprehensive or general exams, and a dissertation all prioritize single authorship at the expense of co-authorship, editing, public writing, curation, media production, design, public humanities, and community work—skills that are increasingly important even within the university. Departments should therefore aim to replace at least one-third of graduate student output with more diverse and transferable forms of intellectual work. In doing so we should think creatively, along the lines of pop-up public art installations or writing action item memos for elected officials, integrating collaborative projects with local businesses into graduate programs and training students to work with big data in ways that are transferable to innumerable other fields, as just a few examples.

5. Freelancing and so-called alternative careers are no longer the exception, but the norm (indicating the limited relevance of the onetime popular "alt-ac" terminology). Training graduate students in grant writing, media production, consulting, and other transferable skills is now essential for the professional success of students and the survival of the discipline.

6. Simply put, humanities graduate (and perhaps even undergraduate) programs must adapt or die—even if only to maintain the modicum of relevance required to stave off department closures.

Specifics: Faculty

1. Acknowledge and share the accomplishments of all of your alums, regardless the careers they create for themselves (i.e., not just those few who land tenure track jobs). This can be done in a variety of ways and at a variety of sites:

   1.A. Create alumni awards that recognize the wide array of professional successes among your alums, to celebrate outstanding work of those working in all post-doctoral settings. Acknowledge alumni who have sustained engagement with the program, such as those you invite back to participate in career workshops or roundtables. Such events highlight the ways alumni use their skills in a variety of careers and contexts, lending substance and thus credibility to what might otherwise may seem like marketing and rebranding claims on the part of the department.

   1.B. Bringing alumni back to talk at an awards event or careers event bolsters the network of contemporary students who are able to ask particulars about what other sorts of work and careers involve, how the alumni moved into that field or industry, how the alumni uses their training and skill sets, and how an interested student may do the same. These events also place interested students in the alumni's own social networks, enhancing the students' visibility.

1.C. Create and highlight alumni profiles on the department's website; in fact, instead of writing lengthy essays about how degrees translate, consider instead listing recent alumni job titles and provide alumni profiles for recent graduates, in other words, show don't tell. Place this list alongside (or combined with) tenure track placement information, to help acknowledge that these are not so-called alt-ac jobs but legitimate professions and careers that your program's graduate training has helped to make possible for onetime students.

1.D. Invite alumni to be in contact with the department once a year to further cultivate a larger sense community, to the benefit of both the alums and also the current students (instill in the current students an eventual responsibility they have to those who will one day follow them in your program). What are they doing now? Where are they working? Consider an alumni reunion outside of an annual conference (inasmuch as professional conferences in the field are likely not rallying points for many of your alums).

2. Bring alums in non-academic jobs back to the program in structured and official ways beyond one-time career events, to serve as mentors, capstone project supervisors, and perhaps even full-time faculty. In doing so, and in recognition of the constraints already on those faculty who may already wish to be part of the solution, departments can enhance their ability to proactively link the skills that are acquired in the program to life and careers beyond the tenure-track. In other words, let those who have become experts in how to apply religious studies beyond the discipline help to shape the future of the discipline.

3. Recognize that graduate training as a job and compensate it accordingly This may mean admitting fewer students in favor of offering a sustainable living wage to those who are admitted, aiming to compensate students relative to or competitive with related entry level professional jobs in teaching, administration, and research. In other words, do not rely on students to supplement their income with loans; loans do not make a doctoral wage livable, given the extended pause in savings, retirement investments, etc., while one is enrolled in graduate school.

4. Address the language problem so widespread in academia, i.e., this is a problem of categorization, with which many scholars of religion are now more than familiar. For example, such terms as "training" or "student" can denote an apprenticeship model that is baked into the whole system and which is no longer credible or viable. Graduate students are currently categorized as "staff" or "student" inconsistently and when it's institutionally convenient (e.g., when it comes time to consider benefits or wage increases). While changing job titles may seem superficial, it has material effects. Determining a new nomenclature will provoke faculty to rethink what it is that students are doing; for if the tenure track religious studies job market will only hold a small fraction of your alum, then what are your current students actually training to do? How else can you categorize their work, especially if so many of them work in careers outside the academy?

5. In making changes to your curriculum, don't over pivot into the logics of the market. Yes, graduate school provides lots of skills that can translate readily and impressively into corporate and nonprofit sectors (see "build a portfolio" below), but if we convert humanities graduate school into "job training" (for some idealized but otherwise undefined future position) then what makes graduate school such a desirable experience for many succumbs to the logics of capital markets. In the best scenario, graduate school is time spent reading, thinking, writing—it is a good life; it does not have to be training for a specific set of next steps if it is a fairly compensated job that helps graduate students to build skills and portfolios for the next step in their career. Very few jobs outside of the academy have such clear lines of career promotion—i.e., there is a treadmill model within the university system wherein one is presumed to advance from graduate school to the tenure track, and from the ranks of assistant to associate, full, and, eventually, the status of emeritus. But this is now a possibility for precious few, and part of the problem the field now faces is one of trying to reimagine the first steps of this treadmill. Reinventing the research degree as job training merely reinscribes the problem; for, outside of academia, a person might take a job for a few years, gain skills, learn more about their strengths, motivations, etc., and move to a rather different job to take on new challenges once they have built a set of experiences and portfolio of work. How can a research degree prepare a student for this sort of professional life?

6. Invest far more in ongoing professional development. Some programs have already begun hosting workshops for professional skills like C.V., grant, and application writing, along with interviewing, peer teaching assessment, etc. But all of these initiatives are part of a model that presumes the doctoral degree is preparation for a career

as a professor. Departments should therefore add additional skills that readily translate outside of the academy, such as creating resumes and professional websites for each student, identifying extracurricular courses that are easy additions to graduate training and which enhance so-called stretch skills.

7. Revise courses so that they culminate in the creation of public portfolios. This entails complementing traditional assignments, like journal publications, essays, etc., with public-facing materials that will help grad students to build professional portfolios of their own. Such new assignments can involve reading notes, blogs, quantitative research findings, etc., that are easily made public and can be included as professional samples that demonstrate skills beyond the usual content expertise which we have long assessed via essays, comprehensive exams, and dissertations.

8. Revise letters of recommendation so that students can use them outside of the traditional tenure track job market. This will require faculty to convert parts of what are more than likely their standard recommendation letters, knowing that parts may be used publicly, such as blurbs that can be posted on LinkedIn, professional websites, etc.

9. Encourage students to become involved in summer internships (on and off-campus) and freelance work—opportunities and professional relationships that the department itself should invest time in establishing (i.e., creating a service role among the faculty for the Director of Internships). Internships, if paid, and such freelance work can boost grads pay, enhance networking, and provide practical experience between academic school years. This, of course, will require supervisors and programs to adjust summer research expectations accordingly. Encourage students to take on paid, professional freelance work early to build their portfolios and work with grad students to understand when something can count in both "buckets"—e.g., writing a journal article, editing or indexing for a senior scholar, designing syllabi for a department are all things that can and should bolster a freelance portfolio, exemplifying specific and tangible skills.

10. Address gatekeeping in the profession and a sometimes common lack of imagination among faculty members and students alike who may fail to understand how the game of academia has changed. The ecology and hierarchy of graduate school places inordinate pressure on students to align with their mentors' interests, choices, and values. If mentors do not believe in success outside of the tenure track, or work to make it possible, this problem (and stigma) will remain.

11. Public scholarship and social media have become a proportionally large part of academic and so-called alt-academic work. The curriculum for graduate training must reflect that. This should include training not only in how to participate in or manage these discourses, but also focus on their history, their power structures, and the ethical complexities entailed in this form of public discourse—all topics on which many religious studies graduate students are already working, though admittedly in different historical periods, regions, and media.

Specifics: Students

1. Learn to identify and communicate the basic and desirable skills that you bring to projects, which means learning how to translate your routine scholarly work for people that are well outside of the academy and who may therefore not take this work for granted. For instance, saying that one has experience teaching, researching, and writing can be broken down into the more basic elements or components of each, such as: "identify and accomplish incremental goals," "navigate and align interests of multiple stakeholders, to find collaborative solutions to problems," "lead and motivate team members in the service of specific tasks," "train and evaluate team members in existing processes and best practices," "survey, summarize, and synthesize large data sets," or "convey findings succinctly to wide audiences in a variety of formats."

2. It's never too early to begin to build portfolios that are exemplary of each of your diverse skills. Just as a C.V. is not necessarily the same as a resume (and knowing the difference is itself a key item), lists of publications you have written, conferences you have attended or courses you have taught are not the same as discrete examples of the work that you have accomplished. To help accomplish this, departments should prioritize the production of tangible, public-facing work that credits individual students for specific roles. Masters-level work, especially, should help students produce freelance portfolios and practice working with teams.

3. It's also never too early to begin to build networks—within the field, yes, but also beyond the field, and especially outside of academia. You may rely on such relationships, and the knowledge gained by working within or moving across fields and professions, far more than you had originally anticipated, whether eventually working in a university or not. Graduate students will be more likely to succeed if they cultivate broad professional networks beyond the university.

4. Practice translating your essays, book reviews, courses, etc., into a form that appeals to, or is more accessible to a broad, public audience

(the so-called public humanities). Use the material on which you are already working to create blogs, write for local papers, etc.—i.e., see each of these as opportunities as ways to expand your networks and to practice writing for and thereby working with a wide readership.

5. Identify what are now sometimes referred to as "stretch skills" (skills that are outside of your current competencies) that pair with your ongoing classes and research, i.e., what can you learn each year that does not overburden your time and energy but which complements your career choices—whatever you end up doing. Traditionally, some academics saw their writing as a vehicle for wider careers in publishing (e.g., enhancing such skills as copyediting or indexing) but today those stretch skills could just as easily involve acquiring the computing and research design skills common throughout what is now known as the digital humanities.

6. Talk with freelancers, alumni, and other community members to understand what kinds of work are possible with the skills that you bring to the table. This can help you to understand how to talk to others about your skills and also what to charge for the kinds of services that you can offer, should freelancing (while a student or as a career later) be in your future.

7. Collaborate and share materials openly and generously with your cohort and networks. Send one another opportunities, edit one another's work (bonus: put that in your freelance portfolio), and continue to ask questions. Celebrate your peers' success.

Postscript: The Bonfire of the Humanities

When a wood cabin catches fire in the winter, it is reasonable to assume that its inhabitants will first try to put it out with snow or whatever is at hand. If that fails, they will quickly try to move their belongings to safety and continue to try to extinguish the blaze. However, if the fire keeps burning still, there may come a point when all that is left to do is to enjoy the fire for its remaining warmth and perhaps cook something in the embers. As scholars of rites and feasts, we may be uniquely equipped to find excess in such disciplinary destruction, able to transform chaos into fleeting joy. But we are hopeful that proactive members of our field, along with those working across the fields commonly collected as the humanities, can intervene well before it comes to this. But such intervention first requires us to smell the smoke and then to realize not just that our house is on fire but that it has been burning for quite some time.

Acknowledgements

Our thanks to Jacob Barrett and Erica Bennett, then graduate students in the study of religion at the University of North Carolina and the University of Alabama, respectively, for their assistance proofing and commenting on an earlier draft of this chapter. This chapter was previously published in *The Bulletin for the Study of Religion* 51/3–4 (2023): 83–92.

Andrew Ali Aghapour earned his Ph.D. at the University of North Carolina, Chapel Hill and is Consulting Scholar of Religion and Science at the National Museum of American History; he is also a comedian and artistic producer.

Shannon Trosper Schorey, who earned her Ph.D. at the University of North Carolina, Chapel Hill, is a Principal Communications Specialist in the tech industry as well as a freelance writer and editor of fiction and nonfiction. Her work has appeared in *The Dread Machine*, *Punk Noir Magazine*, *Machines in Between*, and *Religion Dispatches*.

Thomas J. Whitley earned his Ph.D. at Florida State University, worked in university administration before transitioning to politics and local government; from 2018–2022 he served as the Chief of Staff for John Dailey, the mayor of Tallahassee, Florida, and he is currently the Director of Strategic Innovation for the City of Tallahassee.

Vaia Touna, who earned her Ph.D. at the University of Edmonton, in Canada, is an Associate Professor in the Department of Religious Studies at the University of Alabama, where she is also the Graduate Director for a M.A. program that combines social theory and practical digital humanities skills. She is the author of *Fabrications of the Greek Past: Religion, Tradition, and the Making of Modern Identities* (2017), editor of *Strategic Acts in the Study of Religion: Towards a Dynamic Theory of People and Place* (2014) and co-editor of *Fieldnotes in the Critical Study of Religion: Revisiting Classical Theorists* (2023).

Russell T. McCutcheon is University Research Professor and, for 18 years, was the Chair of the Department of Religious Studies at the University of Alabama. He has written on problems in the academic labor market throughout his 30-year career and helped to design and run Alabama's skills-based M.A. in religion in culture. Among his recent work is the edited resource for instructors, *Teaching in Religious Studies and Beyond* (Bloomsbury, 2024).

Notes

1   We are, however, grateful to the students and faculty—several of whom were from Florida State's program (long noted for providing many of its doctoral students with abundant undergraduate teaching experience)—who attended and also participated in the panel's wide-ranging discussion.

2   On February 17, 2021, the nonpartisan Center on Budget and Policy Priorities observed that between 2008 and 2019 (once it had adjusted for inflation over the decade): U.S. higher ed funding from governments had already decreased by $3.4 billion; thirty seven states cut per-student funding, six of those states by 30% (the average cut was $1,033 [or 11%] per student); tuition at public four-year colleges went up by $2,576 (35.%; in ten states it increased by more than 50%) and at community colleges it increased by $1,098 (37.%). To put a finer edge on this, these numbers all predate the effects of the COVID-inspired recession (see www.cbpp.org/research/state-budget-and-tax/states-can-choose-better-path-for-higher-education-funding-in-covid [accessed March 15, 2022]).

3   Among the early examples that seems to have gone largely unheeded in the field were the essays from over twenty years ago collected together as "Late Capitalism Arrives

on Campus: Making and Remaking the Study of Religion," published in *Bulletin of the Council of Societies for the Study of Religion* 26/1 (1997). For another example from this era, see also Russell T. McCutcheon, "'We're All in this Together': Some Resources for Thinking about Academic Labor," *Bulletin of the Council of Societies for the Study of Religion* 27/3 (1998): 70–73.

4   This has resulted in far more of the costs for their education continually being passed along to students and their families via regular tuition increases over the past decades.

5   According to a 2018 study from the American Association of University Professors, "at all US institutions combined, the percentage of instructional positions that is off the tenure track amounted to 73 percent in 2016." As the report goes on to note: "For the most part, these are insecure, unsupported positions with little job security and few protections for academic freedom" (see Overall Trends at www.aaup.org/sites/default/files/10112018%20Data%20Snapshot%20Tenure.pdf [accessed March 15, 2022]).

6   Of course, there are those in fields largely unaffected by these financial conditions who seem blissfully unaware, as evidenced most recently by a viral tweet, from a geneticist, praising academic work and lamenting the number of colleagues opting to leave for industry. That the thread was tone deaf to the plight of Humanities scholars was made profoundly evident in its many responses. For the original tweet see: https://twitter.com/DrDanielleDick/status/1502288826479398912 (first posted on March 11, 2022).

7   As will become clear, we resist this designation, inasmuch as it still represents careers in academia as the norm and others as "alternatives"; instead, as recommended below, we advise redesigning graduate education as preparing its students for a very wide breadth of careers, only one of which involves seeking positions as faculty members.

8   Without belaboring the point, the Department in which two of the authors work, at the University of Alabama, is one such exception to the rule, inasmuch as it offers an M.A. degree focused on, among other things, digital humanities skills that intentionally prepares its students for a wide variety of professional futures, both within and outside of academia. And we would be remiss not to also mention the M.A. in Religious Studies at Georgia State and its working relationship with their local Wellstar Health Systems as well as such things as their certificate in nonprofit management and concentration on religion and aging. Concerning the last, see the podcast: www.religiousstudiesproject.com/podcast/applied-religious-studies-at-georgia-state-university/ (posted December 16, 2019). The AAR's Applied Religious Studies Committee is also worth noting, though as yet we see no practical or wide effect across the nation from the various "conversations" sponsored by this committee.

9   It should be noted that there are debates around just what "applied religious studies" entails. Given the manner in which the object of study in our field is often taken as self-evident (and thus left largely undefined), the data of the field has sometimes been assumed to have obvious relevance beyond a narrower or more traditional view of the study of religion; this can entail an approach to "application" that assumes the scholar of religion to bring a needed perspective to some seemingly non-religious topic or field, given their expertise in studying such things as myths, scriptures, or symbols, etc. A different approach is to emphasize the methods rather than the content, thereby seeing the wider contribution of the scholar of religion to rest on their skills despite the historic situation, people, or texts and actions where they happen to have honed them during their studies. In such cases, applied religious studies can result in work in domains or careers that would sensibly strike many as having nothing at all to do with

religion. Which of these two approaches is adopted will, to be sure, impact the extent to which the field's training can be applied.

10 Case in point, consider reactions to the 2021 streaming series, "The Chair," in which it was frequently observed that its Department of English was represented as having no adjuncts or graduate students generating the bulk of the credit hour production that largely justifies the existence of such a department today. Instead, the series—as progressive as it was celebrated by some as being (what with having a female Chair who was also a member of a racial minority)—portrayed an outmoded version of a university department (i.e., comprised of tenure-track or tweeded tenured professors) that was more akin to memories of the 1950s than the practical realities of the twenty-first century.

11 The amount of mundane report writing, compliance trainings, grant writing, meetings, as well as professional, university, college, department, and even community service can, for many, be completely overwhelming—all of which is then compounded by the effort to responsibly prepare for classes, engage students outside of class time, while also devoting time to one's own research and publication. That the demands of a personal life and family responsibilities have not even been mentioned should signal what are for many the shortcomings that are now associated with a career that was once widely assumed to be elite and desirable.

12 We think here of Aaron Hughes's plenary address to the 2021 annual meeting of the North American Association for the Study of Religion, which challenged attendees to focus on the rhetoric of crisis itself.

13 Jonathan Z. Smith, "The Introductory Course: Less is Better." In Mark Jurgensmeyer (ed.), *Teaching the Introductory Course in Religious Studies: A Sourcebook*. Atlanta: Scholars Press, 1991, 187.

Responses

Chapter 6

The Future of an Illusion

Barbara R. Ambros and Randall Styers

Reflecting on their experience as the past and current Chair of the Department of Religious Studies at the University of North Carolina, Chapel Hill, Barbara Ambros and Randall Styers offer a reply to the co-authored manifesto that anchors this volume.

Many people are drawn to graduate studies in the humanities because of the distinctive and powerful encounters that occur during their undergraduate years. The encounters might involve charismatic or influential mentors, particular bodies of knowledge, or exceptionally dynamic classrooms. These encounters appear to open up the prospect of a decidedly appealing form of life—a "life of the mind," of ideas, conversation, and writing, a mode of life that can seem far removed from the more mundane and tedious marketplace.

The fantasy of this form of life is a central component of the ideology of the modern liberal university. It is what particular types of college applicants are taught to anticipate, what they are promised in return for exorbitant tuition bills. Given the transitional stage of life of the undergraduate years, a number of students are prone to find exactly what they are looking for, or to convince themselves that they have.

Of course, many faculty members were themselves prey to these ideological dynamics earlier in their own lives. Despite the often-dispiriting conditions of their own current employment, many faculty members still hope to replicate those encounters. To feed that hope, even inadvertently, they shield their undergraduate students from the more unsavory aspects of their professional circumstances. The fantasy surrounding these encounters is fed by an overdetermined forcefield of projection and counter-projection.

In his reflections on religion, Sigmund Freud called these types of dynamics illusions. Freud took care, at least superficially, to distinguish the wish fulfillment that underlies illusions from the overt falsity of delusions, but the differentiation ultimately meant little to him. In the scenario under examination here, the differentiation matters little as well. The fantasy of an idealized "life of the mind" is thoroughly ideological, even if teachers and students share mutual incentives to maintain the glow of that illusion. Many precocious undergraduates apply to graduate programs in the hope of careers that will allow them to recreate those encounters for others through this vision of research, reflection, and mentoring.

In the face of this fantasy, the experience of graduate school has a harshly disillusioning effect. Graduate students are confronted with many of the distasteful realities that were often obscured during their undergraduate reveries. Seminar rooms can be competitive; bodies of knowledge become instrumentalized as strategic resources; and mentors often demand that their students ratify the professor's own life choices and intellectual commitments. Many of the harshest realities students confront in graduate school are economic: their labor in the classroom is woefully under-compensated; debt from student loans can be overwhelming; and the bitter realities of the dwindling academic job market loom ominously. Students see many of their most creative, ambitious, and well-trained peers graduate into the demeaning and unsustainable gig economy of contingent faculty.

We teach at a public university in the United States and are grateful for many of the productive issues and concrete suggestions raised in the manifesto of this volume, particularly since we have close personal and professional ties to several of the authors. The conversation surrounding this intervention has been building for some time in many quarters (in discussions among faculty, at academic conferences, and in professional organizations). As the authors of the manifesto declare, major structural changes in graduate programs in religious studies are imperative, particularly given the dramatic transformations under way in American higher education and the shrinking academic job market for Ph.D.s in the humanities. The following reflections are shaped by our experiences in serving as department chair in a religious studies department at a large public university with its set of particular strictures and policies.

The scenario we open with is far from the only path that brings students to graduate study in the humanities. It is nonetheless useful to consider that scenario because it can shed light on some of the important impediments to change in the structure of Ph.D. programs in religious studies. As we respond to the specific proposals in the manifesto, it is helpful to identify some of those obstacles. We must remember that barriers tend to slow change but do not obstruct it completely. Only with a clear recognition of forces bolstering the status quo can we move forward productively to implement reform. We then propose several strategies to begin addressing the manifesto's call for action.

Impediments to Change

Despite their public image, American universities are notoriously conservative institutions. While academic trends might change at a fashionable pace, any foundational or structural change in these institutions happens only very slowly. University bureaucracies can be extraordinarily hierarchical and entrenched, and as they grow, they make innumerable demands on departments and faculty members. Using an array of bureaucratic tools, they monitor and assess course enrollments (including in graduate seminars), numbers of majors, graduation rates and time-to-degree, teaching loads, and a host of other measures of "productivity." At public universities, political interference in university governance is a constant threat, as politicians see university faculty as coddled, lazy, and ideologically suspect.

Many universities rely on large cohorts of graduate students to maintain undergraduate enrollments, so there is a deep administrative incentive to maintain a healthy pipeline of graduate enrollments. Underpaid teaching assistants and graduate instructors can keep a steady flow of undergraduates moving through the pipeline, while reliance on adjunct and fixed-term instructors can circumvent the long-term commitments of tenure-track positions. Some M.A. programs in religious studies function as profit centers for their universities since many of those students pay significant tuition, often in the hope of one day being admitted into a doctoral program.

These types of economic concerns shape graduate education at every turn. Many departments have extremely limited resources that are woefully insufficient for existing faculty and graduate students. They rely on position authorizations from university administrators, and there are often serious restrictions on hiring, which then slow the process of curricular change. There are pulls in competing directions for the use of limited departmental budgets, which typically need to cover faculty research support, facilities maintenance, and undergraduate programming in addition to a graduate program. When resources are stretched, even the most obvious and desirable objectives—such as maintaining an active and engaged alumni network—can seem difficult and costly (in time, energy, and money).

Many chairs and faculty spend a great deal of time and energy pleading with administrators (and donors) for more funding for graduate students since, even from the most self-interested perspective, the value of stipends determines how competitive a Ph.D. program can be in relation to its peers. Higher stipends can improve living conditions, morale, and the pace at which students move through programs, but decisions about stipend levels and other graduate student benefits are largely beyond the control of department faculty. Inadequate student funding, in turn, exacerbates a host of problems and can breed a range of dire inequities.

What about the faculty mentors? Faculty members themselves spend many years developing particular types of focused professional expertise, and through that process, they are socialized into distinctive sets of professional and intellectual values. Many think of themselves first and foremost as independent contractors; what matters most to them is their own professional agenda and personal success, and they can view their departmental contexts simply as the platform for that career. At the same time, faculty are constantly pressured to excel on the external measures of their productivity for promotions, pay increases, and professional advancement, so their personal research agendas remain central. At the same time, they also have to perform university service obligations, which many see as an intrusion onto their "own work" or their "real work." Given how they are evaluated and compensated, many faculty view service obligations (including such fundamental tasks as undergraduate and graduate student mentoring, committee work, and even independent reading courses) as uncompensated volunteer labor, even though service is contractually stipulated as a specific obligation for almost all faculty.

As a result, many faculty members have little time, energy, or motivation to rethink the structures within which they work or to retool themselves with new skills or capabilities. They are the extraordinarily lucky winners in the academic lottery, but they are easily blinded to their own privilege. As the manifesto makes clear, the same systemic factors that constrain the career possibilities of current Ph.D. students also contort the professional lives of tenure-track faculty. One of the remarkable aspects of higher education in America is the degree to which even the most privileged faculty members can often feel demeaned and undervalued, oblivious to their own institutional and social power.

Beyond this professional myopia, many faculty members are ill-equipped and unprepared to imagine significant professional transformation. They are often unreflective, trained only in a very narrow set of skills and expectations, and unable to teach (or even value) non-academic skills, including public scholarship and fluency in social media and burgeoning new modes of artificial intelligence. The manifesto points out that religious studies faculty have "definitional, descriptive, comparative, interpretive, and explanatory skills." However, many faculty members in the humanities often fail to recognize or identify their concrete methodological skills; they simply do what they were trained to do with little self-awareness or reflection. Thus, many faculty members struggle to explain exactly what they do or why it matters to a broader audience. If these faculty members do actually name or explain their own skills, it is difficult for them to imagine how those skills might be transferred into new professional contexts, especially since so few of them have ever worked in other professional contexts themselves.

As the manifesto explains, graduate training and advising in the humanities are most often built on an apprenticeship model, and even the most critically attuned faculty members can be caught up in that dynamic in a host of ways. They often view their graduate students as apprentices and expect their students to adopt the faculty member's professional methods and values. Many want their advisees to ratify the faculty member's professional values and life choices by replicating those values and career trajectories. Even without the most minimal training in psychology, it seems clear that a great deal of projection can animate these relationships.

Steps Forward

So, what can be said in response to this rather demoralizing set of circumstances? First, as the authors of the manifesto make completely clear, any meaningful change cannot happen just at the individual level. It is not a matter of individual advisors and mentors offering better or different guidance or support for specific cohorts of graduate students. The types of change that will provide a meaningful response to these inequitable and unsustainable problems must be structural, so even as we think in local terms, we must remain focused on broader systemic changes. Higher education in America is already in the midst of a major transformation, and humanities scholars need clear-thinking and persuasive action to counter the market and political forces seeking to commandeer that change. With that perspective in mind, given our experience as departmental administrators, our suggestions for moving forward focus on perspectives and decision-making at the faculty level.

Perhaps the most important step forward is to ensure that all faculty members are constantly reminded of the harsh realities under which their graduate students currently work and the harsh realities of the academic job market. This means that we must actively combat the antiquated, hierarchical apprenticeship model of mentoring. While the most significant initiatives to challenge this model (such as graduate student unionization) remain controversial and unfeasible in many contexts, a sea change must happen in graduate programs to compel humanities faculty to recognize the folly of imagining that current graduate students can replicate their mentors' career trajectories. Faculty must also remain focused on the precarious working conditions their doctoral students face, as so many humanities graduate students provide their universities with woefully undercompensated labor while accumulating imposing mountains of debt.

Next, we must broaden our basic understanding of knowledge production and education. Vital innovation happens through an array of mechanisms and locations of teaching and research, including museums, libraries, archives, academic publishing, research centers, university administration, educational technology think tanks, secondary education, free-lance social media and writing, and more. Humanities faculty typically have little direct experience within the corporate world since many have worked exclusively in academia. While it may be difficult to ask faculty to train graduate students to translate their skills into contexts that faculty members themselves know little about, faculty members can more easily envision these adjacent educational fields since they usually have at least some tangential exposure to these professions through their own teaching and research. This is a first step in pressing faculty to contemplate a broader job market and in beginning to train graduate students to recognize and market their transferrable skills. Based on what we have seen in our graduate program, students often seek these broader educational contexts as they move beyond a narrow notion of academia.

Keeping this expanded definition of education in mind, we must rethink doctoral admissions. It is important for graduate programs to actively seek out applicants who bring identifiable, transferable skill sets to their graduate education and who have career ambitions beyond the academy. For example, applicants who identify their career goals as working for a museum, in academic publishing, or at an archive and who may already have practical experience in these fields are exceptionally well-positioned to understand how to transfer the additional types of skills they will develop in a Ph.D. program in religious studies into these settings. Their faculty mentors will know from the start that they are not fashioning students in their own image and, in collaboration with the students, will have a better sense of what concrete new skills the students might need. These students will, in turn, be invaluable allies of their peers since they can share their perspectives and concrete professional skills formally and informally with their cohort.

We also need to be much more deliberate and intentional in identifying the kinds of transferrable skills we already impart to our graduate students. The manifesto mentions "definitional, descriptive, comparative, interpretive, and explanatory skills," but the specific skills graduate students develop in graduate programs often go beyond this set. Religious studies departments are broad and multidisciplinary, teaching not only methodological and theoretical skills but also a range of skills that are potentially practical (such as archival, archaeological, and/or ethnographic research, various languages, and the craft of writing) and pedagogical (teaching and mentoring), all of which can translate readily into new career trajectories.

Often during orientation for new graduate students in our particular program over the years, we ask our in-coming students to think concretely on the first day of their first semester about the specific set of skills they want to be able to advertise when they go on the job market as they prepare to graduate. What tools do they need to have in their toolkit five or six years down the road? This exercise has been useful in encouraging students to think about the specific set of skills they need to develop and the various ways they can imagine cultivating and demonstrating those skills (coursework, exams, and publications, of course, but also various types of departmental, community, and professional service, certifications, and other extra-curricular activities). But as we have used this metaphor of the "toolkit" with our first years, we have been far too focused on the academic job market. That metaphor seems particularly apt in response to the issues raised in the manifesto since it can help press students and their mentors to identify a much broader set of skills and also a much wider range of ways to foster those skills. It is vital that students begin that strategic planning from the opening days of their graduate education.

Implementing meaningful changes to doctoral requirements and dissertations is challenging given the enormous pressures in many programs to speed the time to degree and the continued need to serve the students who do hope to pursue tenure-track jobs. While replacing a substantial portion of graduate student output with "more diverse and transferable forms of intellectual work" may not be feasible in every case, creating a much broader range of options that could serve students depending on their specific needs and trajectories is essential. Such training can be woven into seminar assignments, M.A. and doctoral exam structures, thesis and dissertation projects, and existing professionalization courses and workshops. Graduate programs must also become willing to consider more fundamental changes to the components of doctoral programs since the structure and requirements of many programs have simply been inherited from earlier generations and seem patently misaligned with the current media and markets through which knowledge is produced and transmitted. By envisioning and implementing these types of changes, programs can serve both students who hope to pursue the diminishing academic job market and those who aim for other career paths.

Economic decisions demonstrate our deepest values, and faculty regularly have important input into decisions about allocating department budgets. Faculty members must reimagine how departments can spend their (even limited) resources to help open new possibilities for their graduate students. Whether this means new types of departmental programming, new internship programs, new investments in student social media presence, or other ways of helping students develop the kinds of professional skills that will help them in the new employment market, faculty must rethink the traditional modes of department programming and activity. Since faculty members are often ill-equipped to train students in these new types of skills, departments will need to turn to outside experts for some of this new programming. The training those outsiders can provide will also be valuable for the faculty themselves as modes of knowledge production and transmission continue to change.

Alumni—both graduate and undergraduate—are an invaluable, often-untapped asset for humanities departments. They are an excellent resource for expanded graduate student training since many have moved into other careers. One important use for department funds can be maintaining active connections with department alumni. With those networks in place, departments can initiate talks and workshops that bring together graduate students, faculty, and alumni in order to expand graduate students' (and the faculty's) sense of the range of employment opportunities and to provide students with a broader network of mentors and professional contacts beyond the academy.

These factors should also shape how departments think about new faculty positions and hiring. When new position authorizations are being discussed, graduate faculty should identify the particular types of skills that new tenure-track faculty can bring that would provide concrete benefits to future graduate students, not just in the more traditional academic skills but also in areas signaled in the manifesto: public-facing scholarship, social media, and other non-academic skills and professional experience that can benefit students. Tenure-track job advertisements often ask for the impossible, but maintaining attentiveness for potential faculty members who can bring added, and unexpected, value to graduate programs can enormously benefit students.

Faculty members are also members of larger academic and professional communities. They participate in university governance, professional organizations, conference planning committees, political organizations, and other networks of scholars and citizens that have crucial roles in thinking about the future of higher education. As we think about systemic change, it is vital that faculty members carry the values we are considering here into those new contexts. It is risky for an individual graduate program to restructure the nature of Ph.D. requirements on its own, so the broader profession must rethink what constitutes adequate credentialing and what counts as merit and productivity. Professional organizations must expand their notions of programming and professional training. Conferences need to include new types of knowledge-making and new modes of presentation. Faculty members must also become vocal and aggressive opponents of their employers' reliance on undercompensated labor, whether from graduate students or the contingent labor force.

Graduate education in religious studies has been enthralled by many illusions over the years. Those illusions have always been a murky product of fantasy and projection, but these illusions have increasingly direct harmful effects on some of our most engaging and creative students. We might not be able to dispel all of those illusions, but we must be willing to recognize the fundamental shifts in the social and economic contexts of our profession. In those changing contexts, we must rethink the foundational aspects of our relations to our graduate students, our understanding of professional training, and our vision of what counts as scholarship.

Barbara R. Ambros is a Professor and Chair in the Department of Religious Studies at the University of North Carolina at Chapel Hill. Her research on Japanese and East Asian religions focuses on gender studies, human-animal relationships, and place and space.

Randall Styers, a former Department Chair, teaches Religion and Culture in the Department of Religious Studies at the University of North Carolina at Chapel Hill. His research focuses on the cultural history of the study of religion and religion in various aspects of American law and culture, particularly such topics as gender politics and debates over the relation between religion and science.

Chapter 7

A Response to the Manifesto

David Frankfurter

> Reflecting on his experience in the Department of Religion at Boston University, David Frankfurter offers a reply to the co-authored manifesto that anchors this volume.

I think we can all agree that a declining academic job market, the widespread cynical shift of college teaching positions to insecure adjunct posts, and a concomitant decline in doctoral applications (as intelligent college graduates assess the dismal landscape) all demand a rethinking of humanities Ph.D. programs. I can really only address Ph.D.s in the history of religions, which involve an even more recondite series of skills (linguistic, historical, textual) than the Manifesto envisions in the religion doctoral status quo.

But let's think first, and sympathetically, about the principles and benefits of the old model, which was alive and well when I began my graduate studies (1984). You would be accepted into a doctoral program based on your languages, your control of an historical period or range of texts, your ability to articulate a promising interest area, and some spark of creative insight that suggested you could carry yourself through "the archives." Once accepted, you would then be trained more deeply in philological, historical, and theoretical inquiry so that you could contribute something original and substantive to the greater knowledge of religions in history—to *Wissenschaft*. You would learn how to present your ideas in publication—the dissertation serving as a principal exercise in this skill—and you would learn (somehow) to develop and teach fascinating undergraduate courses. (If there was mention of alternative careers en route, it would be a gesture to library science or even ministry—the latter a horror to many of us).

Once hired, you would continue your research contributions to the field and thus bring credit to your college or university, which would support you (minimally) with sabbatical leaves and occasional fellowships. You might also shift your work to emphasize public engagement. You might find that the institution that hired you (e.g., a small liberal-arts college) preferred you to focus on teaching excellence more than research and publications. Still, even those institutions want to see you attending conferences, publishing contributions, and generally interacting with the world of *Wissenschaft*. Advancing scholarship was really the goal for everybody, the doctoral student, the professor, and the university patrons. Exciting the undergraduates was also a goal, although that varied in the 1980s and 1990s.

This was the system that lay behind the history of religions Ph.D. And I think it is important not to dismiss it out of hand, even given the realities observed in the Manifesto (and even acknowledging a fundamental but inevitable elitism in this system). We should not dismiss it because—as individuals, as a culture, and as people in history—we all value knowledge and expertise. We want to know that there are folks out there who know about human sacrifice in Ireland or priest-hoods in ancient Babylon or folk religion along the Silk Road. (I got a call this summer from a science journalist who wanted my take on an ancient Egyptian jug with residues of hallucinogens. He thought it was a great story but needed someone with expertise to make sense of it). That knowledge and expertise does not come from learning how to write for newspapers but from interacting with the archives—with recondite publications and artifacts.

The Manifesto, it seems to me, entirely misses this historical and cultural role for expertise borne of esoteric academic engagement in the interests—it seems—of educating people instead with broad educational abilities. But don't we, as a culture, crave proper authorities? Especially in an anti-vax, conspiracy-ridden period of American history? Let me give an example of one of our most accomplished Boston University religion Ph.D.'s, Andrew Henry, who runs the well-known video series "Religion for Breakfast"—a premier example of the "alternative career." Indeed, it has served him, his life-choices, and the view-ing public very well. For those who have seen Henry in his broadcasts, he has an exceptional knack for making complicated texts, artifacts, and ideas about the history of religions exceptionally clear. But as his dissertation advisor I also know how he prepared for this successful experiment in public engagement through his philological, epigraphical, textual, and historical training. In fact, his disser-tation remains a brilliant contribution to the field. I don't think—and I doubt that Henry thinks—that he could have produced "Religion for Breakfast" with simply training in public scholarship. He presents himself gesturally, verbally, and in choice of content as a scholar, an expert.

My larger point here is that, in dispensing with the "tradition" of the "monograph-length dissertation" (#4), setting aside the mandate to work and publish within recondite archives in order to find one's original academic path, and fronting "high-quality public scholarship" as the most worthy goal while encouraging alternative academic careers, the Manifesto is really designing a high-quality Masters program, not a Ph.D. program. Once one sets aside all of the things that bring field expertise and that train people to contribute to *Wissenschaft*, there is really no more reason for a Ph.D. at all! The sorts of alternative careers to which graduate training in religion can contribute—public and international ser-vice, grants organizations, media, social work—would be (or should be) entirely open to graduates of effective three-year Master's programs that aspire *beyond* random coursework and university name-recognition. Master's programs could be rigorous, competitive among each other for training students and for securing diverse career placements for them. Why reconceive the Ph.D. when the skills called for in alternative academic jobs are not doctoral-level skills?

Indeed, at no point in the Manifesto are the reinvented skills and training justified as worthy of a doctoral degree. Doctoral students in the traditional model should *also* learn about alternative career paths without prejudice, should *also* compile teaching portfolios, and should *also* learn about grant-writing and media production (an expansion of the process that consequently puts even more pressure on students trying to gain expertise in a field of knowledge). I think that many American graduate programs in religion are already moving in that direction. Boston University's Graduate Career Development program offers, e.g., humanities summer internships at museums, libraries, and local government;[1] while the religion department's required "professionalization seminar" spends a week on alternative careers, bringing in outside speakers. Employment of doctoral students in religion is a very live issue. But to reinvent the Ph.D. in religion to eliminate the dissertation and what it accomplishes, to substitute public engagement for gaining and communicating expertise, that all seems to me to turn the Ph.D. into an M.A.—an excellent M.A., to be sure, and one that should be promoted, but certainly not a doctoral program.

What then do I think will happen to the Ph.D. in the history of religions? As a graduate supervisor I see fewer and fewer acceptable applicants, which means to me that fewer students with unique intellectual capabilities for doctoral study are choosing it. Yet this does not mean that the *Wissenschaft* model I laid out in the beginning is outmoded, for there will always be new texts discovered, new theoretical models to be applied, new archaeology, and new discoveries in the archives themselves; and those novelties will need expertise, not just *National Geographic*. With fewer doctoral students, perhaps some universities will close their Ph.D. programs in religion entirely, but that does not mean those programs should have continued in a public-scholarship, dissertation-free guise. It just means that there will be fewer people engaged in doctoral-level scholarship for the time-being.

David Frankfurter is Professor of Religion and Aurelio Chair in the Appreciation of Scripture at Boston University. A specialist in Ancient Mediterranean Religions and Early Christianity, he is the author of *Evil Incarnate* (Princeton, 2006), *Christianizing Egypt* (Princeton 2017), and (editor), *Guide to the Study of Ancient Magic* (Leiden 2019).

Note

1   See   www.bu.edu/humanities/opportunities/graduate-opportunities/Ph.D.-internships/reflections-by-interns/ (accessed August 24, 2023).

Chapter 8

In the Best Scenario ...

Martin Kavka

> Reflecting on his experience as the current chair of the Department of Religion at Florida State University, Martin Kavka offers a reply to the co-authored manifesto that anchors this volume.

Manifestos are usually sets of demands to readers, based on a clear account of what has gone wrong and what the necessary solution is. The authors of Chapter 5 have written a manifesto that meets these criteria. To us, faculty in programs in the study of religion that offer graduate degrees, the authors demand a curriculum that is more public and more portable. The problem is that we faculty have so often been mired in the past. We assume that we can train others in the way that we were trained, and that means that our programs graduate people at the M.A. and Ph.D. level who have some arcane knowledge but are completely unprepared for an academic job market that fails to acknowledge the value of that knowledge, by having a sufficient number of openings for tenure-track jobs in the study of religion, and are also unprepared for a non-academic job market since our graduates have only academic skills. The solution, for the manifesto authors, is for us faculty to acknowledge that time has passed. We must now train our students differently. They must imagine audiences that are truly public, beyond the professors who give them grades and write recommendation letters on their behalf. They must gain other skills that are portable to non-academic careers. They must integrate their alumni who now hold non-academic positions not only into their department's networks, but even perhaps hire them into academic positions so that religious studies can thrive beyond its disciplinary boundaries.

Some faculty who read this manifesto will fall, dismayingly, into the temptation to cavil. They will ask how we might verify that any work that addresses the public is actually heard by it. Since two of the authors of the manifesto are faculty members at the University of Alabama, perhaps one might ask about the uptake on the "Uncivil Religion" website that their colleague Michael J. Altman developed along with several of their graduate students and the Smithsonian's National Museum of American History. (How many hits? How many citations?) They might ask how they are to gain the ability to teach these portable skills, given that institutions do not support the retraining of faculty, and there is no guarantee that a significant portion of current faculty will show facility with various digital-humanities applications and platforms. They might complain that adding these new elements into the graduate curriculum can only lengthen students' time to degree. But administrators at various institutions are already complaining about how long it takes to get a Ph.D., and some M.A. programs are trying to compact their two-year programs into one-year programs in order to attract applicants.

All of these cavils have ready responses, and one doesn't need to be a department chair to construct them. In addition, the caviler's oppositional stance doesn't do a single !@#$ing thing to address the genuine problem that the manifesto authors raise, which is that the humanities in North America are structurally dependent on cheap labor (graduate-student teaching) in a way that forestalls the expansion of the more expensive professoriate.

Nonetheless, I want to call attention to something going on in this manifesto that strikes me as atypical. For the authors want advanced degrees in the study of religion to be more geared to market realities, more useful, while they also have a deep affection for what they take to be the *uselessness* of the study of religion and the humanities in general. This is clearest in the fifth of their specific demands:

> In making changes to your curriculum, don't over-pivot into the logics of the market. Yes, graduate school provides lots of skills that can translate readily and impressively into corporate and nonprofit sectors ... but if we convert humanities graduate school into "job training" (for some idealized but otherwise undefined future position) then what makes graduate school such a desirable experience for many succumbs to the logics of capital markets. In the best scenario, graduate school is time spent reading, thinking, writing—it is a good life; it does not have to be training for a specific set of next steps if it is a fairly compensated job that helps graduate students to build skills and portfolios for the next step in their career.[1]

In the best scenario, graduate school leads to a life of pleasure that cannot be reduced to market forces. And this best scenario is not some phantasmatic ideal; anecdata suggest that many tenured professors still hold substantial nostalgia for the comparative innocence of graduate school and the time spent reading and thinking with others, even though they may have been accumulating debt and struggling to pay rent at that time. The authors of the manifesto who hold non-academic positions then simply want what non-precarious faculty at colleges and universities already have: a life that is to a substantial degree beyond markets, simply because it involves the pleasures of communing with oneself and others, pleasures that cannot be monetized and that suggest a personal growth that cannot be reduced to economic growth. They recognize us privileged faculty, and they recognize that what we have is good. Indeed, their talk about the desirability of graduate school in humanities—and I assume in the study of religion—is continuous with descriptions of religious-studies students when the field was expanding markedly in the 1960s. As Robert Michaelsen, the founding chair of the Department of Religious Studies at the University of California Santa Barbara, wrote in 1966 about the popularity of religious-studies classes, "Many observers have noted that this student generation is far from being apathetic. Students are interested in issues and concerned about decisions in areas vital to them. Many of them wish to strip away the frills and to get down to the elemental issues of life."[2] Michaelsen did not talk about pleasure per se, but insofar as he counterposed the study of religion to the way of the world, the authors of the manifesto are here extending his rationale for the study of religion, and for humanistic study in general.

I confess to being somewhat surprised by the manifesto on this issue. I don't necessarily remember my own move up the promotion ladder as part of the "good life" that the manifesto authors imagine. I have shown some talent at reading, thinking, and writing during my career, but I have rarely taken joy in that talent. It takes me away from others much of the time, and chains me to my keyboard. Thoughts regularly enter my head: "Why am I reading this? Are these thoughts any good? If I write something, will anyone ever pick it up?" Teaching rarely calms me, simply because my power over my students (I assign them grades) means that I cannot always trust their responses. Whatever reading and thinking and writing I do on top of my administrative tasks as department chair comes piecemeal and often seems disjointed, since emails require prompt replies; meetings have to be arranged and they always seem to start just before I've figured out how the next paragraph in my writing should run. My nostalgia for graduate school isn't a nostalgia for the content of my coursework and dissertation. It's a nostalgia for a time when coursework and dissertation-writing weren't interrupted by other things; it's a nostalgia for simplicity.

The problem with the recognition that the manifesto authors extend isn't simply that I believe they are misunderstanding the nature of academic privilege and its good life to some degree. It's that the role that pleasure plays in their analysis threatens the logic of the entire manifesto. The academic life is one of pleasure, they say, *but they refuse to say that too loudly*. The call for more transferable skills in graduate education is the dominant narrative voice in the manifesto. In the one paragraph that they mention that being a graduate student can be a "desirable" life, they admit that transferable skills are not their only, or perhaps even their main, desire. Skills, and the earning potential that they provide, are one desire. Pleasure is another. They seem not to be able to imagine both coexisting. Oddly, the authors of the manifesto who now hold non-academic jobs do not break out of the collective authorial voice to talk about the pleasure of their non-academic careers. They only ask that faculty acknowledge their careers as "legitimate." It is as if they chose skills over pleasure. They too have their wistful nostalgia, as they implicitly ask those of us who train graduate students to prepare them for less pleasurable lives.

Perhaps I have misunderstood them, as they have misunderstood me. Indeed, I suspect that all their lives contain moments of intense professional pleasure. I know this for a fact in one case. In the summer of 2022, I interviewed Thomas Whitley, one of the manifesto's coauthors (and a graduate of the program in which I teach), for a feature in the Spring 2023 department newsletter about undergraduate and graduate alumni working in local politics. I asked him how his time in the graduate program affected his work as chief of staff to Tallahassee's mayor, in effect hoping for a quote that would affirm to the newsletter's readers that my colleagues and I indeed were passing on portable skills. Here is part of his response, focusing on his experience teaching the department's introductory survey of religious traditions:

> While thinking about what my students should get from that class, I didn't want to teach them facts that they would forget in six months and look up on Wikipedia later. I wanted them to learn about claims of authority, power dynamics, sex and sexuality—larger concepts—and tie that into asking the right questions. That's important in politics too. My time in the department also taught me to talk about what we do in a way that matters to other people. Teaching is a kind of translation, and during my time in the mayor's office, we took complex policies and explained them to random people on the street, telling them about how those policies would improve their lives.[3]

There are several pleasures that Whitley invokes here, it seems to me. One is simply the satisfaction taken in improving both students' and citizens' analytical skills, and the kind of consensus that that can produce. Another seems to lie in the consensus that such improvement can produce. When we justify to our students why the questions we ask of a tradition, or of the problematic concept "religion," are useful questions—when we show them the intellectual benefits of the lingo of the study of religion—we are on the same page with them. They are our partners in inquiry. We trust each other more. More people speak, and that improves the life of the classroom. A third lies in the continuity between working for our students and working for our fellow citizens. If teaching is about a kind of "translation" for Whitley—a change in orientation or lingo that reaps benefits either in getting better answers when one asks more sophisticated questions, or in improved quality of life as a result of a policy that might seem jargony at first blush—then his role in Tallahassee politics bears formal similarities with his teaching role as a graduate student. For him, the pleasures of the classroom have fed into the pleasures of his public life in Tallahassee.

The authors' manifesto rarely mentions graduate-student teaching. It insists that giving teaching experience to graduate students is one of many "entirely inadequate developments" in graduate training in the humanities.[4] Nonetheless, we know that at least one of the manifesto's authors saw his teaching while a graduate student as a kind of job training. It is the case, as the manifesto's authors claim, that departments need to broaden the skills that they give their students. As they say, "traditionally, some academics saw their writing as a vehicle for wider careers in publishing (e.g. enhancing such skills as copyediting or indexing) but today those stretch skills could just as easily involve acquiring the computing and research-design skills common throughout what is now known as the digital humanities."[5] While the traditional skills they invoke are still marketable—I think of two recent graduate students in my department whose work assisting faculty in editing scholarly journals led them directly into positions in state government or in university staff—new ones should be added, even if they have to be acquired through coursework in another department. That being said, the traditional skill of teaching is also marketable, and it is this that I want to add to the manifesto authors' recommendations: we should talk about teaching differently. Teaching is not simply, or even primarily, about passing on content, as Whitley rightly notes. It is about shaping a student's voice, making it more compelling, developing its agility so that it can respond on the fly to others around the table, and as a result maximizing its authority both in the classroom and in later workplaces.[6] In addition, one should regularly describe teaching not only in the highfalutin' language of preparing tomorrow's thinkers and leaders, but in its everyday gruntwork. Teaching is a kind of project management. In delivering learning in a classroom setting, an instructor decides on the scope of a class session and semester, sets a schedule and sticks to it, controls the quality of the class, selects resources, communicates well (and constantly), manages both the negative and positive risks of various pedagogical and grading strategies, and perhaps procures outside speakers, all the while maintaining the engagement of the students who are among the key—but certainly not the sole—stakeholders in the course's success.[7] This is project management in a nutshell; the only thing lacking is budget management.[8]

I do not know whether a faculty member at an institution classified by the Carnegie Foundation as "R1: Doctoral universities—very high research activity" can say in public, without risking his job, that teaching is the most important thing that happens on his campus. But certainly such a faculty member can say that it is a central thing that happens on his campus. Given the portable skills that Whitley has rightly associated with teaching, it strikes me that we who train doctoral students should reframe how we see teaching in our own departments. An instructional assignment for a graduate student is not simply an excuse for that student to collect a stipend. Leading discussion sections, which comprises the majority of instructional assignments in the Department of Religious Studies at the University of Virginia and other institutions, is not simply a time for graduate students to review and clarify professors' lectures. Being an instructor of record, which comprises the majority of instructional assignments for doctoral students in my own department and other institutions, is not simply a way for those students to bring enrollment dollars into a department by offering the same course at a time when a faculty member is unavailable. Grading is not simply mindlessly giving checkmarks. Teaching is *the* thing that graduate students do that hones their most portable skills, their project-management skills that are as valuable as the ability to program in Python or R. We faculty should take that seriously, and take our responsibility to increase the attention we pay to training students as teachers.

That means at least the following. Departments of religion and religious studies that train graduate students must build at least one course about pedagogy into the graduate curriculum. When graduate students meet with faculty in colloquia, there must be regular opportunities for graduate students to talk about, and workshop, their experiences teaching. Faculty must observe graduate-student instructors and section leaders regularly, and write detailed reports on those observations. (My institution requires that observations be done only once a year, and does not require any written report that would show that a faculty member has actually given feedback to a graduate student. That is laughable.) They should check in with graduate-student instructors and section leaders on top of observations. They should give dissertating doctoral students the option to develop their own class and teach it, and work with them closely both in preparing that class and implementing it. In short, faculty members' assignments of responsibilities should include a substantive and robust percentage devoted to teaching supervision.

In such a department, faculty teaching loads would not decrease. That is not how large institutions, or at least the large institutions that have employed me, work. But faculty research loads would. And they should, especially (but not necessarily solely) for tenured faculty.[9] The manifesto authors rightly decry the research demands made of doctoral students, which privilege the arcane over the useful. With that I am in full solidarity; I only make a small addition to their recommendations, on the basis of the knowledge that when the manifesto authors have taught, they have been at their most useful. Their teaching is an integral part of the best scenario of graduate education.

Martin Kavka is Professor and Chair of the Department of Religion at Florida State University. Now in the twilight of his career, he is most proud of his editing work, including (with Aline Kalbian) a decade as coeditor of the *Journal of Religious Ethics* and (with Anne Dailey and Lital Levy) the volume *Unsettling Jewish Knowledge: Text, Contingency, Desire* (University of Pennsylvania Press, 2023).

Notes

1   A. A. Aghapour et al., page 55, this volume.

2   Robert Michaelsen, "The Study of Religion: A Quiet Revolution in American Universities", *Journal of Higher Education* 37.4 (April 1966), 185. This essay was reprinted the following year in *Religious Studies in Public Universities*, ed. Milton D. McLean (Carbondale: Southern Illinois University Central Publications, 1967), 9–14.

3   T. Whitley, "Department Alumni in Local Politics: Thomas Whitley," Florida State University Department of Religion newsletter (Spring 2023), 7. The newsletter is available online at https://religion.fsu.edu/sites/g/files/upcbnu446/files/media/files/newsletters/newsletter_2023_spring.pdf.

4   Aghapour et al., page 50, this volume.

5   Ibid., page 58, this volume.

6   My views about teaching are deeply indebted to thoughts about the liberal arts and their function that I first heard from my former colleague Laurel Fulkerson, who began her career at Florida State University as an assistant professor in Classics and retired in 2022 as Vice President of Research. For a distillation of her views on the liberal arts, see "The President's Symposium: The Future of Higher Education," www.youtube.com/watch?v=J1LfCDr-8qQ, 28:56–34:38. At the end of those remarks, she echoes Whitley's comments about translation.

7   The list of what goes into a classroom is adapted from the chapter headings of Andrew Ramdyal, *PMP Exam Prep Simplified* (New York: Technical Institute of America, 2021).

8   Graduate students who work on conferences or symposia during their careers gain budget-management skills too. But that has little to do with networking with guest speakers. Instead, those skills are learned in what can be the quite complex act of ordering and delivering food to attendees.

9   There is much to say here about the research requirements associated with faculty in humanities fields gaining tenure at R1 institutions. In short, I think they are too high, and the demand for "the tenure book" perversely associates expertise with the thirtysomething scholar over the sixty-something scholar. In addition, the economics of humanities publishing and college/university library budgets can no longer support the book as a sine qua non for tenure.

Chapter 9

The Way We Lived Then and Now:
The Ph.D. and its Employments

Richard A. Rosengarten

Reflecting on his experience as both the past Dean of Students and also the Dean
of the Divinity School at the University of Chicago, Richard Rosengarten offers a
reply to the co-authored manifesto that anchors this volume.

I am grateful for this manifesto and to have this opportunity to reflect with
it. I propose to do so comparing the present moment to which the manifesto
responds, with past initiatory moments that have marked by own professional
life. Fully half of that life has been spent in academic administration where without question a major, if not the controlling consideration of that work has been
doctoral education in relation to the academic job market.

So my gratitude is inflected with a certain fear and trembling that what follows
may make me sound like some sort of Qoheleth figure, harumphing that there is
nothing new under the sun. That is not my intended rhetorical position. Rather
it is to suggest that what is particular to our moment is a familiar if especially
emphatic manifestation of what has been true in the academy for decades. Its
address thus requires us to distinguish between the constants of contemporary
academic life and its specific manifestation in this moment. I hope to map out a
semblance of that territory. Doing this will inevitably be autobiographical, and—
like all reflection on these topics, I've learned—inflected by institutional context.
That is where we all start, especially on a topic like the relationship of placement
to training within the Ph.D for the study of religion.

I matriculated as a graduate student in the Department of English at the
University of Chicago forty-four years ago, in late September 1979. The department's orientation lasted one half of the Friday preceding the start of classes on
Monday. It consisted of two events: a meeting with my academic advisor to select
my courses for the autumn quarter, and a session with a panel of five Ph.D. students
who on their own recognizance had convened the approximately twenty-five of
us M.A.s aspiring to doctoral study to inform us that there were no academic jobs
to be had, and to counsel us to reconsider our decision to matriculate.

Their message reiterated what I had been told the previous fall by my college
professors from whom I'd requested letters of reference. To a person they told
me directly and emphatically that there was not a future in the academy. After
my rudimentary orientation to the English department I learned, over beers at

the Woodlawn Tap in Hyde Park, that my new M.A. colleagues had had similar experiences with their college teachers. Despite this chorus of foreboding spanning quite varied contexts, the unmistakable (if a bit boozy) consensus around the table was that we were where we wanted to be, and excited to start doing what we wanted to do.

I received no financial support for that first year so I needed a job. I was hired by the Director of the University's Office of Career Counseling and Placement Services, Julie Monson, to support her goal to create a program to encourage Ph.D. students to consider careers outside the academy. Ms. Monson assigned me two tasks for the 1979–1980 academic year: (1) to interview faculty across the campus to ascertain the degree to which they were (or were not) attentive to this question, and (2) to write, in consultation with recent Ph.D. graduates who had taken up careers outside the academy, an in-house manual (titled *Your Plan B*) to rehearse how they might make alternative plans for their professional lives. My notes from those meetings, and my draft of *Your Plan B*, were handed off to my successor, a full-time, salaried staff person (interestingly not, if I recall correctly, the holder of a Ph.D.) who was hired the following June to carry forward this program on a full-time basis.

A coda to this rehearsal:

- Of the five Ph.D. students who cautioned us not to seek Ph.D.s because there were no jobs, three completed their degrees, secured tenure-track positions, have had productive careers in teaching and research, and are now contemplating retirement. At least one—the one who has the highest public profile—has continued to write actively and with a mix of urgent agitation and stern admonition about such issues as adjunct faculty, enforced retirement, and the vagaries of life in the academic-industrial complex. Two eventually withdrew from the program, one to work in consulting and the other to direct a writing program. I am sure that concerns about the job market informed the decision of one of them, if not both.

- I lack reliable data on my twenty-five M.A. colleagues from the 1979–1980 school year, in part because I left the English department to do my Ph.D. in the Divinity School. Over the last four decades I have run across five or six of them who hold tenured academic appointments. Two of the twenty-five were admitted to the Ph.D. program in English at Chicago, and each of them secured a traditional academic appointment and is now completing a career in the academy.

- The most inspiring aspect of my job at Career Counseling and Placement Services was meeting Ph.D. graduates (from the late 1970s) who were working outside the academy. The three who made the strongest impressions were humanists: a historian of Ireland who was running an international survey for the American Public Works Association; a scholar of comparative literature who had gone into student services; and an art historian who went to work for a major advertising agency. Of these three, one tried and could not secure an academic job, the second was persuaded he would not and did not make the effort, while the third had decided over the course of her Ph.D program that she did not want to be in the academy. Irrespective of field or outcome, each spoke without rancor or regret, indeed with appreciation and affection, for their doctoral work. None expressed even a modicum of discontinuity between their doctoral training and their career; indeed each articulated relief about a happiness that they suspected they might not have felt had they pursued a tenure-track position. They were receptive to the idea of encouraging students to cultivate a "Plan B" but to a person noted that this was not what they had done.

- Faculty whom I interviewed responded quite variously to the idea of graduate students having or cultivating a "Plan B." I encountered some bemusement and a little hostility to the idea. Most of those I interviewed were senior scholars, which in 1979 meant that they had obtained their doctorates in the 1950s. Nearly all were male, and most were married to someone who assumed responsibility for much if not the entirety of domestic life. Everyone acknowledged and understood the issues of the job market. That said, there was no real consensus about the extent of its severity; and the idea of addressing it explicitly engendered dubiety at best and suspicion at worst.

This rehearsal and coda aim to underscore that academic employment for Ph.D.s has been a major issue from the moment I took my initial steps toward an academic career forty-four years ago. That status of the matter has never abated. This constant needs to be part of our collective reflection in this moment. The problem the manifesto addresses is of the longer rather than the shorter term. It is also inflected by differences in available jobs among subfields within the study of religion (about which more below).

None of this ameliorates the brute economic realities of higher education: in the past decade, the budgetary calculus of increasing enrollment, decreasing full-time faculty, and relying on adjunct teaching has inexorably increased. I rehearse the history both to exhort the greatest possible realism about circumstances for new Ph.D.s—and not incidentally to account for the fact that, in the midst of these vagaries, the number of Ph.D. programs has increased and student interest has at least remained steady, if not increased.

So we need to frame our situation, and I propose to do so by contrasting the systemic with the idiosyncratic, where "the systemic" is what we might posit to be generally true about employment and Ph.D. programs in religion over the last four decades and "the idiosyncratic" is our best assessment of what is true about those matters in 2023. The goal is not to accept the systemic as absolute, or to presume to address with comprehensive precision the idiosyncratic; rather, it is to afford in their juxtaposition a perspective on the here and now.

The following is thus a rough and ready sorting of what I am terming the systemic and the idiosyncratic:

Systemic	Idiosyncratic
From the perspective of the university, financing Ph.D. students is not only not budget neutral but an outright cost.	Ph.D. student funding must be linked directly to their teaching of undergraduates, which does not eliminate but will help to ameliorate the cost.
Supply of Ph.D. students seeking academic employment exceeds institutional demand (especially when the latter is restricted to tenure-track teaching appointments).	Growth in the number of Ph.D. programs has created an exponentially larger supply of Ph.D. students at a time when demand is quite unevenly distributed.
No Ph.D. program ever places 100% of its graduates in tenure-track appointments.	Few Ph.D. programs are placing more than 50% of their students in tenure-track appointments.
Ph.D. programs consist of three academic components: coursework, exams, and the dissertation.	Ph.D. programs consist of those three components but have introduced a range of other considerations that at a minimum run parallel to and often inflect those components, usually under the rubric of "professionalization."

The systemic column offers a set of "constants" for the relation of Ph.D. education to academic employment, while the idiosyncratic column attempts to articulate how those constants manifest in our moment. It begins by acknowledging that funding doctoral education in religion (I would say, in the humanities and social sciences generally) is not "budget neutral" for universities: in blunt budgetary terms, it is a cost. This has always been true. What varies over time and place is how institutions regard that cost, and how (if at all) they allay it. At present, universities chiefly recover that cost by having Ph.D. students teach classes. This allows the schools to matriculate more undergraduates without increasing the number of tenure-track faculty they employ. It is tempting (and not merely wrong) to see the university as Leviathan in this; less often acknowledged but also not merely wrong is that the emphasis we currently place on pedagogy as essential to doctoral education plays directly into the "pay to play" approach to doctoral education. It also not incidentally serves to reduce available tenure-track jobs.

So far as I know the supply of Ph.D. graduates has exceeded the hiring potential forever. It is thus more helpful to think about the extent of the disparity and its location. I can speak more directly about what Chicago has experienced in this regard; but that news collates broadly with data provided by the American

Academy of Religion and the Council on the Graduate Study of Religion. The major points are these:

- There was an overall reduction in academic placement beginning in the late 1980s. There are a variety of hypotheses for why this happened, some more intuitive than others but none, so far as I can see, probative.

- In response to this, nearly all the larger Ph.D. programs reduced the size of their Ph.D. cohorts. (Chicago reduced by half, from approximately 370 to 185.).

- There was a period in which the overall percentage of Ph.D. students securing academic placement did decrease, but that decrease stabilized at a level only slightly lower than had been the case previously. (This is a subtle point and perhaps the least well recognized aspect of our topic.)

Two other important factors inflected the placement situation at this time. First, a number of universities inaugurated new Ph.D. programs. This increased the supply of Ph.D.s seeking academic employment. Second, at the same time theological schools and seminaries that had employed Ph.D. graduates for decades began to shrink in both number and size. This shrinkage diminished the demand for Ph.D. graduates, especially in such fields as theology, ethics, and the history of Christianity.

Extra-institutional factors, chiefly social and economic, also influence placement in specific moments. After September 11, 2001, demand for scholars of Islam ratcheted up considerably. So far as I know, no school training scholars in Islam saw its graduates who wanted academic jobs have any difficulty in doing so. At Chicago we witnessed both this development and, at the same time, a strong demand for scholars of Judaism, and (carrying over from the previous decade) a somewhat diminished market for graduates who had concentrated their studies in theology and ethics. (We did not witness a diminished market for scholars in biblical studies—see J. Z. Smith on the place of the bible in the study of religion.).

A less "field-specific" but crucial inflection occurred with the financial crisis of 2008 and its aftermath. This created a state of (at best) suspended animation in most institutions with ostensible hiring needs: elimination or "non-renewal" of positions, the displacement of tenure-stream appointments with term appointments, etc.

Returning to our table of the systemic and the idiosyncratic, the common denominator in graduate programs' response to the dynamics discussed above has been to place an ever more explicit emphasis on training in pedagogy for doctoral students. The change here strikes me as at once subtle and crucial. It is also emergent, so that what follows is to some degree speculative.

At least at Chicago, teaching has been, certainly since the 1980s, a part of almost every Ph.D. students' life. Until very recent years, however, it was informal rather than formal. The "network" of Chicago students who taught at schools such as

Loyola, DePaul, Saint Xavier, the city colleges, etc. was, and to some degree still is a well-worn path for doctoral students. What has formally replaced that is a program of seminars and tutorials on aspects of teaching (lecturing, leading discussions, writing syllabi, etc.) and an array of practical experiences: tutoring in the university's Writing Program, serving as a Teaching Assistant in undergraduate and master's-level courses, and stand-alone teaching of a class in the College's core curriculum. Sufficient emphasis is placed on this program that students select a faculty mentor to help them to shape this experience.

None of these arrangements address a major component of the "Manifesto" in that they do not (at least directly) prepare students for careers outside the academy. While I am not (so far, at least) persuaded that replacing the informal "network" of teaching with a "pedagogical program" is an improvement, I'm also not sure that the inclusion of "extra-academic" experiences geared toward non-academic employment would add particular value for Ph.D. students who either do not succeed in obtaining or decide they do not wish to pursue academic employment.

My dubiety on this matter stems goes back to my interviews some forty years ago with Chicago Ph.D.s who did not enter the academy. None of the trio described above brought any professional training whatsoever to the "non-academic" profession they entered. All judged that the training the Ph.D. gave them in writing and research was crucial to their success in their "alternative" career. Not only did they express "no regrets" about pursuing the doctorate; they were grateful for the skills it inculcated and saw a direct link between those skills and their successes in their professional lives. So emphatic was their unanimity on this point that it became the core thesis of *Your Plan B*: do a strong, academic doctorate in the confidence that it will prepare you not for one but for many careers.

On this point I would make strong common cause with what I take to be the manifesto's exhortations that we in the academy need to be more avid and forthright in the case we make for the intrinsic value of what we do. I would simply add as a corollary to this compelling thesis that by implication this indexes a fundamental confidence in the value of the humanities generally, and the study of religion in particular.

It is standard these days to note the scant support of humanistic learning in American society, and I am a full-throated singer in that chorus. The important *caveat*—less acknowledged, in my experience—is the failure of nerve of many scholars when the question of "impact" is raised. We as a group are quick to privilege the contemporary over the historical in response to the demand for "impact"—a process that, it seems to me, cuts off our nose to save our face. We live in an impatient cultural moment, but we practice disciplines that are, at their core, about patience. If we do not show the discipline of patience, we do not show our true selves to a world that very much needs it; and we forfeit that most basic identification to those who are all too ready both to tell us who we are, and indeed who we should be.

If, as the manifesto suggests, we are in a moment when this is precisely the issue for scholars of religion, it behooves us to be declarative about the value of what we do. I mean that constructively, not skeptically. Particular aspects of our idiosyncratic moment merit our concerted attention. There is also a concomitant truth that undergirds that moment: the humanities in general and the study of religion in particular have suffered from a failure of nerve about their intrinsic value. If my career as an administrator and educator across these decades has one consistent article of faith, it is that those who are thoroughgoingly educated in the study of religion have done, can and will do a variety of things—including, but by no means limited to, teaching and research.

This may run against the core of much conventional wisdom. This moment for all its specificities is still a moment in which our best recourse is to double down on the intensity with which we pursue our particular skills as scholars. My personal conviction is that this does not mean an exclusive emphasis on "theory and method" and its concomitant, specialization: it means instead that these endeavors, however worthy, in fact serve to render the study of religion less rather than more accessible to intelligent and interested people (including students). To the degree that the manifesto emphasizes this, I am fully and gratefully behind it.

Richard A. Rosengarten is Associate Professor of Religion, Literature, and Visual Culture at the University of Chicago Divinity School, where he served as Dean of Students (1991–2000) and Dean (2000–2010, 2015–2017).

Afterword

Emily D. Crews

When I was in the final stages of dissertation writing, I had significant trouble sleeping (a problem likely familiar to many readers of this volume). At night, well after my computer was closed and my head on my pillow, my thoughts and anxieties remained wide awake. At such times I often went against the firm advice of sleep specialists and scrolled around the internet on my phone. One night I came across an ad for a museum curatorial position that sought candidates with expertise in precisely the topics and methods I studied. As a fan of museums of all kinds, I was intrigued by the idea of working as a curator. Add to that the fact that the job was in the city I loved and already lived in and had the same kind of flexibility and creativity that drew me to academia. A few days later, my brain curdled by lack of sleep and cinematic images of myself doing whatever badass things it is that museum curators do, I decided to apply for the job. I had no real plans to leave academia, but I figured I'd follow the advice of all those alt-ac blog posts that circulated on Twitter and "see what's out there."

A few weeks later, much to my surprise, I was offered a first-round interview and, when that went well, a second, more in-depth one. I was even more surprised when I was eventually offered the job. After some agonizing professional discernment (and more sleepless nights), I decided that I wasn't ready to leave academia; I took a two-year post-doctoral fellowship instead (the only other job I applied to that year). Even so, the experience of applying for the curator position, from writing the cover letter to articulating my skills and interests in the interviews, gave me the first inkling that I might be both qualified for and interested in non-faculty positions (who knew?!). What's more, the realization that there *were* jobs out there and that someone might hire me for them left me with a sense of real professional possibility—such a contrast to the scarcity and seeming randomness that characterize the academic job market.

The next year, during my first year of the post-doc, the Martin Marty Center for the Public Understanding of Religion, at the University of Chicago, decided to hire an assistant director as part of an expansion of its ambit and operations. I was invited to apply for that position. Without the previous experience with the museum curatorship I suspect I wouldn't have even considered it. But the more I thought about the job, the more interesting it seemed to me. It offered the opportunity to make use of my doctoral education, but in ways that most faculty positions wouldn't. It came with financial and geographic stability at a time when both were increasingly needed. And it meant that I could set a research and programming agenda for an organization that was growing where so many others seemed to be shrinking.

I was offered the job and, after I completed the first year of my post-doc, I made the transition to the Marty Center. Although the quick pace and many of the tasks were foreign to me (What is an org chart? What do you mean, we don't deliberate about this decision for weeks? Aren't we going to discuss how this works in theory?!), I enjoyed it immensely. The work was challenging and exciting, my colleagues were excellent collaborators, and I was given free rein to develop projects that emerged out of my own research interests and grandest ambitions. Even more, I was drawn to the ethical aspect of public-facing scholarship, which insists that knowledge and the means to produce it be shared with collaborators beyond the walls of our elite institutions.

Still, on the advice of my doctoral advisor and others, I decided to take a stab at the academic job market. It seemed reasonable that I shouldn't close down the possibility of the kind of career I had been trained for and that, for most of my time in graduate school, I had imagined I would have. However, after considering offers for faculty positions at other institutions, I chose to stay at the Marty Center, where I was promoted to Executive Director in the summer of 2023. In this role I set the overall mission and vision of the Center. I collaborate and manage partnerships with colleagues across the university and the city of Chicago, support the Divinity School's faculty and graduate students in translating their work to public audiences, and build relationships between the Divinity School and journalists, organizers, artists, and policy makers. In collaboration with our faculty co-directors, I also craft the research agenda for the Center, which at present focuses on themes like art and religion and religion in Chicago.

Like many of this volume's contributors and others who now hold non-faculty or non-academic positions, I don't regret pursuing a Ph.D. I treasure the years I spent in the classroom, the archives, and the field and am grateful for truly excellent preparation to become a research scholar. Nonetheless, that training did very little to help me to discern whether I might be suited to positions beyond the professoriate, much less to articulate why I might be a sound candidate for them. And although in my current job I use many of the skills I learned in graduate school, there are countless others it never even occurred to me I might need or even just want to know (N.B.: I'm still rubbish at Excel).

The manifesto that stands as the central text of this volume takes individual stories like mine (which shares strong similarities with three of the manifesto's authors) and extrapolates them to generally applicable suggestions for Ph.D. students, recent graduates, and program administrators. Were my own institution to take up some of those suggestions, our current students would be much better prepared than I was to connect their doctoral training to the kinds of non-faculty careers that the majority of them will likely have (whether they embrace that trajectory, as many of us have done, or choose it out of necessity and/or desperation).

It is clear from most of the responses offered that a robust adoption of the manifesto's suggestions (or others like them) is neither compelling to nor even possible for many deans, department chairs, or program directors. As Barbara R. Ambrose and Randall Styers note in their response, this is understandable, to some degree. Senior scholars were taught to be (and to teach others to be) researchers and sometimes teachers. They did not sign up to teach grant-writing or project management or digital media strategies—or to value those skills in the first place. But given the employment crisis in the humanities and social sciences that this volume so effectively characterizes, it seems foolish and, dare I say irresponsible, not to at least consider ways for students to gain more diverse and professionally flexible skills during their Ph.D.s. (I note here, with appreciation, the hopeful tone and context provided by Richard Rosengarten's piece, particularly the characterization of certain current job market statistics as acute expressions of more general truths.) Otherwise, what will doctoral degrees become? Two rather objectionable possibilities I can imagine: vanity projects for smart, wealthy students who don't need to bother about future employment or products of exploitative systems that promise a future to most that is, in reality, available. Only to a very few. There are many, of course, who would argue that the latter is already an accurate description of doctoral programs.

In the spirit of the manifesto's denaturalization of the customs, traditions, and classifications of current doctoral programs and contra the resistance apparent in some of the responses, I want to use the remainder of this piece to share two related sections of practical commentary. First, I want to offer a list of suggestions for doctoral students who find themselves in the same position I did: aware, suddenly, that non-faculty positions might be necessary or desirable, but with no sense of what to do next. Much of the content of my suggestions will echo and hopefully amplify the comments of others who wrote for or whose interviews are included in this book. Second, I want to take a cue from the response offered by Ambros and Styers, of the University of North Carolina, and share some ways the Marty Center might take up the charge of the manifesto.

Practical Strategies for Doctoral Students

1. Stop Thinking of a Non-faculty Career as a Failure

For much of my graduate training, the only career that felt both meaningful and realistic to me was one in academia. "Why would I spend a decade training to be a researcher and teacher only pursue a different career?" went my thinking. This singular significance of the faculty position was underscored at every turn—by my peers, my teachers, the institution, and the field. Anything less than a tenure-track position (preferably one at an elite research university like the one in which I had been trained) was failure. I want to note here that many people who hold this view do so in ways they think are kind and understanding. Most would acknowledge the impossibility of the job market, the statistical realities of supply and demand, the idiosyncrasies of committee preference, etc. And so, as I outlined above, it was pure happenstance that I found and applied for a job that helped to fracture this narrative for me, but I am deeply grateful that I did. It meant that, even when I *was* offered a tenure-track position, I was able to accurately appraise whether it was actually the right choice for me, rather than the one I thought I was supposed to make.

As Pamela Gilbert said so well in her interview at the beginning of this book, the way you evaluate your options and make decisions in your (possibly early) twenties will necessarily look different from when you're near the end of your degree, when you may have student loan debt, family obligations, and other desires and needs related to age and life-course. The idea of moving to a rural town elsewhere in the country, living far away from extended family, or being unable to build financial security "hits different," as my students would say, when those realities are on your doorstep.

For these and so many other reasons, it is essential that we alter our perspectives on value, labor, and fulfilment. This can, of course, be extremely difficult. I don't deny that being unable to pursue the career you have spent years preparing for can be painful, particularly in an industry that so fervently inculcates vocational awe. Many who weren't able to attain faculty positions are forced to confront significant amounts of disillusionment, regret, and grief (not to mention crushing student loan debt). This is an emotional and material reality that very few of our graduate programs even acknowledge, much less provide resources for managing.

This kind of reorientation can also be difficult for current students and recent graduates. Your mentors are tenured or tenure-track faculty and are thus invested in the system that upholds their significance. They may not have either the experience or the incentive to think beyond that model. It is imperative, then, that you stop looking (solely) to your faculty advisors for the kind of advice and approval necessary to make this transition. It is wonderful and affirming when it exists—something I can say from first-hand experience, having had generous, supportive mentors—but it is rarely sufficient. Instead, it's important to surround yourself with people who already take for granted the value of non-faculty or non-academic careers. Learn from people who have made the transition—follow them on social media, read their work, reach out to them if you feel comfortable. Look for a mentor or conversation partner who will affirm, support, and perhaps even aid you in your professional discernment and growth.

Academia is a fascinating industry where one can do exciting, principled, meaningful work. It is not, however, the *only* industry in which one can do exciting, principled, meaningful work. Knowing and acting on this reality is a necessary part of a successful transition to non-academic careers (and recognition of it wouldn't go amiss even for those who do take faculty positions).

2. Start to Think of Your Academic Work *as* Work

As several of the interview transcripts in this volume argue, an essential aspect of the successful transition into a non-faculty career is being able to think of—and then describe—your academic work as just that: work. Being in a Ph.D. program can feel interminably infantilizing, particularly in gerontocratic institutions that refuse to acknowledge that doctoral work is labor and doctoral students are engaged in the full business of a career. Nonetheless, in the years you have been in a doctoral program, you have gained industry-transcending professional competencies that you should learn to articulate in non-jargony language. Some of these are obvious: research skills, including the ability to analyze and synthesize large amounts of data; narrative and technical writing; proofreading and editing; the ability to meet deadlines, self-manage, and complete projects that have multiple stages and may go on for years.

Some competencies are less obvious, however, but are no less significant. Being a productive member of a classroom or a Ph.D. cohort can be described as skill: collaborative work. Teaching and conference presentations can be phrased as strengths: public speaking and audience development. Managing TAs or directing independent studies: personnel supervision. Applying for funding for research or travel: grant writing. Conceiving the scope of your dissertation, serving as a research or editorial assistant, or planning a conference or running a workshop: project management. Maintaining a healthy working relationship with an advisor and dissertation committee over a number of years: proficiency at managing complicated, sometimes difficult, colleagues. (This last one is meant as a joke ... kind of.)

I'm not, by any means, suggesting that you should claim to have skills or knowledge you don't possess. Experience securing grants to support your research is not the same as being a grant writer. But do learn to emphasize the knowledge and abilities you've gained that might not be obvious on a traditional academic C.V. or when you articulate your professional training as, for example, "expertise in comparative exegesis of medieval and early modern Christian scriptures."

3. Take Advantage of Opportunities for Non-academic Training

There is undoubtedly significant pressure on doctoral students to focus on the completion of their degrees. Work that "distracts" from such progress is often discouraged by advisors or program directors, sometimes for good reason. Nonetheless, taking the time to gain additional skills that make you competitive for careers outside academia is vital. This approach is especially the case if you already know you're aiming for non-academic positions, but can also contribute to your scholarly work in surprising ways.

Many universities now offer internship or shadowing programs for graduate students. If time and circumstances allow, take advantage of these. Find out what kinds of opportunities are available through your university's graduate student service office. Look for courses or certificate programs that focus on topics that will build your resume for work in other industries, like project management, organizational design, or digital media and content creation. Likewise, LinkedIn and other professional networking and portfolio sites offer free or low-cost trainings or webinars that can develop some of the same capacity building.

Part-time work or volunteer positions also offer some of these benefits (though I recognize that there are factors that make such work difficult). During my time in graduate school I was an editorial assistant for *History of Religions*, the flagship journal in my subfield, as well as the editor of one of the Marty Center's online magazines. I learned the field in vital ways through this work, but I also gained skills and experience that I regularly use in my role as Executive Director of the Marty Center.

4. Develop a Professional Network

Most scholars I know shudder when they hear the word "networking." In academia, we often approach the concept with suspicion or derision—it seems corporate, self-serving, even mercenary. But it doesn't have to be. When I use the term networking, I mean the act of creating and expanding a series of inter-connected professional relationships in order to achieve a more fulsome sense of your professional life. Having fruitful, mutual relationships with people who understand the concerns of your particular profession or who can give you insight into and opportunities in another is useful and affirming.

How does one network? To be clear, I'm not advising that you start passing out business cards and trading favors. (In fact, I will admit that I myself only got business cards for the first time this year [2023] and have as yet failed to take them out of their very nice box.) Rather, get to know people in ways that come naturally to you or are easily accessibly—conference presentations or steering committees, collaborative work, non-profit boards or other kinds of volunteering, professional affinity groups or extra-curricular social groups. Take advantage of your university's alumni network and reach out to others from your field who have gone into non-academic work. Join conversations that other students or recent grads are having about these same issues. Create a profile on LinkedIn and connect with others.

Being in a university setting is a gift when it comes to exploring new careers. Universities, especially large ones, are tiny cities unto themselves, with people in countless types of jobs working alongside one another. At my own university, for instance, there are offices or divisions devoted to development and fundraising, alumni relations, data management, marketing and communications, publishing (books, journals, magazines) and bookselling, student services, financial management, and more. Don't be afraid to reach out to people who have a position that looks compelling to you (at your university and, of course, beyond). Ask them if they have time for a brief "informational interview"—a Zoom call or coffee meeting in which you learn a bit about their professional day-to-day in order to know whether the same kind of work might be interesting to you. Although it may seem strange to many of us who have spent most of our careers in the academy (I found the suggestion bizarre when it was first offered to me—wouldn't the person think I was rude or nosy if I asked to meet out of the blue?!), in most other industries this is a taken-for-granted practice. Use it to your advantage.

5. Consider Public Scholarship

Many academics, possibly including some contributors to this volume, think of public scholarship as an unserious, insufficiently rigorous, non-academic endeavor. I couldn't disagree more. Public scholarship is academic, in the same way that teaching is academic. Public scholarship *is* scholarship. It is the creation and dissemination of specialist knowledge gained through extensive study, but translated into language and idioms that make it available to non-experts.

The kinds of argumentation and language that make for successful public scholarship also make for strong self-articulation and legibility outside academia. Being able to describe your professional experience in clear and concise language—the so-called "elevator pitch"—is crucial to finding success in non-faculty positions, in the same way that sharp, succinct writing is crucial when writing for the public. What's more, good public scholarship requires the ability to think critically about one's own work and field, to affect and make sense of a position outside one's own, to write with discipline and humility, and to balance nuance with simplicity. These abilities will be valuable in any industry, particularly if you are able to use your public writing as an opportunity to discuss those soft skills in cover letters and interviews.

Conclusion: Manifesto at Marty

By way of conclusion, I want to borrow the approach taken by Barbara R. Ambros and Randall Styers of the University of North Carolina in their response to the manifesto, in which they laid out some ways that they would take up the manifesto's challenge in their own context. I should first acknowledge that, like Ambros and Styers, I recognize that no research center and/or its director can fix the massive structural problems that bedevil the humanities and social sciences. However, I do think that there are ways that an organization such as my own can offer small, measured support to students and recent graduates. Below are three of those things to which I commit the Marty Center in the years to come.

1. Recognition of Student Labor

In their response, Ambrose and Styers write, "Faculty must ... remain focused on the precarious working conditions their doctoral students face, as so many humanities graduate students provide their universities with woefully undercompensated labor while accumulating imposing mountains of debt." Centers can do the same. In moments where it is possible and welcome, the Marty Center and its staff can acknowledge the complicated material conditions under which students do their work. Further, we can support and encourage that work in ways that do not exacerbate pre-existing issues. For example, we can offer students opportunities for meaningful labor that is fairly compensated in a diversity of ways—financially, of course, but also in terms of recommendations, mentoring, C.V. building, and network building.

2. Student Capacity Building

Centers can be excellent places for helping students to gain abilities and experience that they may not learn through coursework and research. From event planning and data-processing to web design and program management, centers require a wide array of skills and knowledge to function well. This volume's manifesto has encouraged me to further collaborate with Divinity School faculty to enrich students' professional development through trainings and partnerships that originate from the Marty Center's pre-existing projects in digital technology, media and public scholarship, organizational management, and exhibition curation.

3. Expanding and Diversifying Spaces for the Production of Knowledge

In their response, Ambrose and Styers argue that doctoral programs must commit to broadening their "basic understanding of knowledge production and education" by rethinking where and with whom such production can and should take place. Although they are, in some ways, on the periphery of graduate education, centers that focus on research and programming are unquestionably spaces where "vital innovation happens." At the Marty Center, it has been our privilege to welcome students as partners in innovation and to empower them to understand our work together as part of their professional growth. Thinking creatively about new ways to undertake such efforts will be foremost in our future planning.

Emily D. Crews is the Executive Director of the Marty Center for the Public Understanding of Religion at the University of Chicago Divinity School. She earned her Ph.D. in the History of Religions from the University of Chicago Divinity School and uses historical and ethnographic methods to make sense of the ways that religion, gender, and the reproductive body are entangled in the formation of personhood.

Appendices

Appendix 1

Tracking Doctoral Graduates in the Study of Religion

Russell T. McCutcheon

Given the sometimes wide and contested understanding as to just what constitutes the study of religion—a longstanding issue in the field[1]—determining how many doctoral students graduate each year and who then look for employment as faculty members can be somewhat difficult; for a lack of agreement on what the field is means that it is not generally agreed which doctoral programs count as training students in the study of religion. What's more, perhaps in part because of such internal identity debates, the field remains misunderstood and, to a degree, marginal in higher education, with some faculty and administrators across (even publicly-funded) campuses continuing to presume that it is a form of Christian theology or even an extension of ministry programs—which goes for organizations producing annual statistics in higher education. Thus, the designator "religious studies and theology"—phrasing long favored by the American Academy of Religion (AAR), the U.S. field's largest and thereby main professional association which has a well-known "big tent approach"—is sometimes assumed to be a useful umbrella term, though one that explicitly conflicts with how many scholars of religion understand and practice the field themselves, in both their research and their teaching/supervision of graduate students. Add to this how the study of religion can often be grouped together with philosophy, possibly because of the once widely accepted (though recently critiqued) assumption that religiosity is constituted through beliefs which supposedly animate their secondary behaviors (e.g., rituals) and social organizations—an understanding of our data that presumably fuels views on the natural alliance between these two otherwise distinct disciplines.[2] And at worse, "other humanities fields" is sometimes used by reporting agencies to group together newly credentialed scholars of religion with large numbers of other program's graduates (possibly those known as area studies), such as those reports that instead focus mainly on such disciplines as English, history, foreign languages, etc., adding the miscellany of "other humanities fields." Accordingly, finding precise and reliable data on the number of doctoral students who graduate each year in the study of religion (and who are, presumably, then on the market for an academic job, what with so-called industry or governmental/NGO options being less numerous than in many other fields), is a very real challenge to those trying to assess the current academic labor market let alone chart a way forward.

Perhaps the most reliable U.S. data derives from the co-sponsored report of the National Science Foundation (NSF) and National Center for Science and Engineering Statistics (NCSES), specifically Table 3.1 "Research doctorate recipients, by detailed field of doctorate: 2021–22" of their annual Survey of Earned Doctorates (SED).[3] For example, there we learn that, for 2021 and 2022, the following number of U.S. doctoral graduates are reported (based on the discipline's CIP code, i.e., Classification of Instructional Programs—a classification system first developed in 1980 by the U.S.'s Department of Education's National Center for Education Statistics [NCES]):

Field of Doctorate	2021	2022
Philosophy and religious studies (total)	598	642
Philosophy	406	432
Religion/religious studies	125	140
Philosophy and religious studies nec*	67	70
Bible/ biblical studies	71	90

* Not elsewhere classified (nec)

Given the above-noted ambiguities in understandings of the field, it would be unwise to assume that the 125 and 140 self-reported doctoral graduates in religion, for 2021 and 2022 respectively, along with the 71 and 90 in biblical studies for these two years,[4] let alone whatever portion of those in philosophy and religion reported by the institutions themselves (i.e., the nec category), are reliable numbers; an unknown number of annual graduates may, at least according to some members of the field, not be understood as scholars of religion eligible for employment in, for instance, a public university's Department of Religious Studies. But, for the sake of argument, we can overlook this variable for the time being.

In addition, the NSF Survey of Earned Doctorates (SED) reports,[5] among many other items, historical trends for doctoral degrees conferred in our field annually over the past decade (once again accepting their understanding of what constitutes this field of "religion/religious studies"). For instance, consider the following doctoral degrees awarded per year in religion/religious studies (row 1) and in Bible/biblical studies (row 2):[6]

	2010	2011	2012	2013	2014	2015	2016	2017	2018	2019
Religion	282	312	290	301	292	314	254	310	258	226
Bible	97	103	95	106	86	87	62	84	113	102

What we can glean from this (to whatever extent, flawed for the above reasons) data is that the number of doctoral students in religion has decreased to a low in 2022 that is 55.4% less than the historic high within the past 13 years (i.e., 314 graduates in 2015) while a significant drop in those earning Ph.D.s in biblical studies occurred several years ago, by 2019 it had climbed to an above average number (the decade's average is 93.5 graduates per year). The reasons for the religion numbers dropping are surely numerous, but are more than likely linked to certain major factors: funding challenges within graduate programs (due to cuts on their campuses, which are themselves linked both the changing campus priorities as well as wider government cuts, such as those in force due to COVID-19 protocols on campuses across the U.S.) that have forced programs to decrease the number of students admitted annually (especially if their desire is to fully fund all incoming students) along with the increasingly widespread presumption among potential applicants concerning the challenges that they will likely face eventually securing full-time employment as faculty members after a potentially expensive and often long period earning the doctorate degree. To rephrase, to what degree this decrease was planned or coordinated by doctoral programs (i.e., in an effort to limit the supply of qualified applicants in a setting in which the demand for their skills as tenure-track faculty members on university campuses has decreased steadily) is questionable. For at present there is no evidence of any such coordinated or field-wide proactive action among graduate schools. The wider job availability in a host of Christian theological institutions across the nation for those variously defined as biblical scholars, notably those trained to work in settings well apart from the public university, may well account for the relatively steady—at least over the course of that decade—bible studies degrees awarded. (Further discussion of this data appears in Appendix 2.)

Postscript: As per Appendix 2, it should be noted here that a very traditional understanding of the study of religion and the role of/training involved in a Ph.D. in this field are presupposed in the data drawn upon and reported in Appendix 1. As such, few, *if any*, of the doctorates annually earned in the study of religion proactively equip students to secure futures outside the university. As exemplified earlier in this volume, what was once called alternative career success is, at least up to this point in time, achieved largely by the hard-won experience, resolve, and entrepreneurial attitude and actions of graduates reinventing themselves upon graduation (or, as is more often than not the case, after several unsuccessful years on the academic job market). Lacking redesigned curricula and requirements that prepare doctoral students for a variety of futures in which their advanced research, critical thinking, and writing skills are relevant and sought, the linkage of data reported in Appendix 1 and the limited opportunities discussed in Appendix 2 remains natural and necessary.

Russell T. McCutcheon is University Research Professor and, for 18 years, was the Chair of the Department of Religious Studies at the University of Alabama. He has written on problems in the academic labor market throughout his 30-year career and helped to design and run Alabama's skills-based M.A. in religion in culture. Among his recent work is the edited resource for instructors, *Teaching in Religious Studies and Beyond* (Bloomsbury, 2024).

Notes

1 This is exemplified by the field's various, and sometimes competing, designations, from Religious Studies (preferred in North America) or the history of religions (the anglicized version of prior German designations that's still favored at the University of Chicago, such as the *Religionsgeschichtliche Schule* associated with Ernst Troeltsch in the late nineteenth and early twentieth centuries or the broader term *Geschichte der Religion*) to comparative religion or comparative religions (the plural is of significance to some), the science of religion, the academic study of religion and, now, at least for a small sector of the current field, the critical study of religion.

2 Collapsing these two fields into one department is, on some U.S. campuses, a well-known practice that dates back many years, often with the study of religion being more of an after-thought or supplement to the better established but, at times, equally marginalized field of philosophy.

3 Find the site at https://ncses.nsf.gov/pubs/nsf24300/data-tables (accessed September 20, 2023); this data is gathered through an annual web-based survey of graduates and institutions.

4 Given that in the U.S. these two major fields rely on the same jobs advertising service, biblical studies numbers (also reported in the SED), are here combined with those in religious studies, to ensure that this graduate data is of relevance to information contained in Appendix 2.

5 Find their customizable search/table generator tool at https://ncsesdata.nsf.gov/builder/sed (accessed September 20, 2023).

6 These numbers are drawn directly from the already prepared table 13 at https://ncses.nsf.gov/pubs/nsf21308/data-tables (accessed September 20, 2023).

Appendix 2

SBL/AAR Position Advertisements, 2001–2019

Russell T. McCutcheon

The longtime collaboration between the Society of Biblical Literature (SBL) and the American Academy of Religion (AAR)—the U.S.'s two largest professional association of scholars in our field—resulted in the creation of *Openings* in 1985 (the once half-size newsprint publication that, for some time now, has been a password protected website run by the SBL/AAR). *Openings* replaced *TOIL* (*Teaching Opportunities Information Listing*), the publication of the Council of Societies for the Study of Religion (CSSR—originally known as the Council on the Study of Religion [CSR], it was founded in 1969 but then disbanded in 2009) and was the onetime umbrella organization to which many North American academic societies in the study of religion (broadly conceived) once belonged, providing member services to each along with two publications (e.g., the *CSSR Bulletin* [reinvented by Equinox, post-2009, as the *Bulletin for the Study of Religion* with the University of Alabama as its editorial home] and *Religious Studies Review* [now owned by Wiley with Rice University as its editorial home], along with an annual hardcopy *Directory of North American Departments*). Established in 1972, *TOIL* itself replaced the AAR's prior placement listing (known as the Academic Referral Service).[1] North American employment information in the study of religion—now listed on an AAR/SBL site simply called Employment Services—is therefore limited to an annual tabulation of positions that have been advertised at the SBL/AAR site (as opposed to tracking successfully completed hires) in the admittedly wide area of biblical studies, (generally Christian) theology, and religious studies. It is important to note that annual jobs reports seem only to have begun to be published by these organizations in 2010, with a report from that year covering the prior decade, followed then by annual reports that end with the 2019 hiring season (the report was posted in the summer of 2020, prior to the beginning of the Fall when the vast majority of ads are posted for positions intended to begin in the following academic year); in private communications with both organizations, the absence of recent statistics is linked to re-prioritized staff responsibilities in both associations due to COVID-19 remote protocols (the annual data is said to exist and so we look forward to seeing reports that cover the COVID-19 and post-COVID-19 hiring years).

Based on the available data,[2] Figure 1 represents the number of discrete open positions advertised via the employment service from 2001–2019, broken down into those that were tenure-track and those that were contingent. That this online jobs site is not the sole resource for advertising faculty positions in

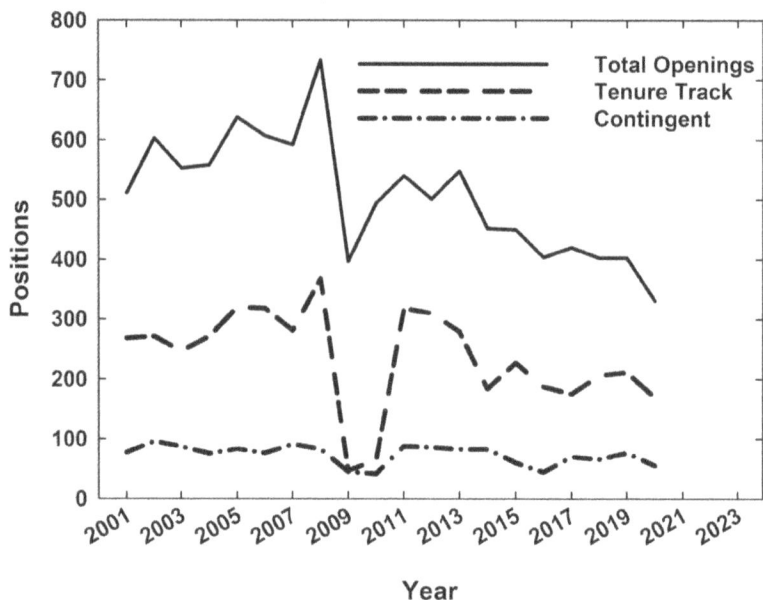

Figure 1. Positions advertised via SBL/AAR.

the North American in the study of religion should be noted from the outset, of course, although it is more than likely the default source for North American departments which, on occasion, is supplemented by duplicate postings at such other sites as *The Chronicle for Higher Education* or, as in recent years, the online site *Inside Higher Ed* in the U.S. and *University Affairs* in Canada. Additionally, it must be noted that the sum of all positions advertised annually (more on this immediately below) obviously exceeds the total of just these two subcategories (i.e., tenure/ tenure-track and contingent) since many positions well outside of traditional faculty lines are also regularly advertised through this site e.g., positions that are: administrative, ministerial, chaplaincy, seminary librarians, postdocs, etc.—a fact that makes plain some of the longstanding institutional and theoretical complexities of this one academic field.

Concerning the point just made: according to the 2001–2010 report (which employs far broader categories than more recent reports), 21.7% of all open positions advertised for that decade were classified in theological studies, 0.5% were in ministry, 0.4% were in Jewish studies, 2.4% were in libraries or a non-teaching center, while Biblical Studies accounted for 4.5%, and 10.3% were in joint philosophy/religious studies units. Among the other remaining fields and subfields listed (e.g., English, history, Middle or Near Eastern studies, etc.), religion or religious studies amounted to 1,868 of the classifications for all open positions during that decade (more on this below), or the expertise required of 39.1% of the positions advertised. Jumping forward, of the 331 advertised in 2019–2020 alone (the most recent report currently available—a year typical of others, though the overall downward trend in openings means that, generally speaking, the numbers are lower than in previous years for each category), 32 were listed as administration or support services, 21 were in Christian ethics, 22 were in Christian studies, 35 were in general Christian theology, 19 were in practical Christian theology, 12 were in systematic theology, 17 were in interreligious studies, 6 were in missiology, 17 were in pastoral care, and 11 were in preaching—making evident how the total number of positions advertised each year is hardly a fair representation of the positions actually available to scholars of religion trained to work in a public university (i.e., those not matching the SBL/AAR's exceedingly broad tent understanding of the field). Of note is that, in that same year, lacking a biblical studies category in the report, 15 positions were listed in biblical languages, 36 were in Hebrew Bible/Old Testament, 43 were in New Testament, 6 in Rabbinic Judaism, 6 were in Second Temple Judaism, and 2 were in Septuagint Studies. Important to note in all of this is that the Position Fields of Expertise (Table 12) itemized in the 2019–2020 report totals to 950 positions, almost three times the number of ads recorded in the report's Figure 1 for that year's total positions (i.e., 331, which is the basis for the above graph's entry for total openings for the final year). Undoubtedly, each position advertised can be classed in more than one area of specialty, given the sometimes breadth of a position (e.g., a position in Christian origins being listed as New Testament but also early church history, perhaps, or a social theory of religion position on women in Asian religions being listed as social sciences as well as a regional or historical designation associated with Asia along with the designation women's studies in religion). This results in the same opening registering more than once when it comes to reporting on its (perhaps various) areas of expertise. (More than likely there is no consistency to this across all positions, of course, with some who list these positions checking just one and others several boxes.)

As is evident from the above commentary, the data included in each annual report varies to some extent, e.g., there is no general religion/religious studies grouping in the more recently reported expertise data; instead, it is broken down into the various sub-fields that, depending on one's definition of the study of religion, may or may not be included in this field. This variation makes a precise analysis of the employment trends challenging, especially given the historical data inexplicitly varying. For example, the 2001–2010 report records that there were 553 positions advertised in 2003, to pick but one year. Yet the number for this same year, when included in the historical data in subsequent reports, is listed instead as 525 in the 2011–2012 report, 519 in the 2012–2013 report, and 538 in the 2014–2015 report. For the purposes of the above graph—intended to represent overall employment trends in the study of religion—the statistics provided in the initial 2001–2010 report have been used for those years, which are then supplemented by the following annual reports' data for each year from 2011 to 2014, and then, for 2015–2020 period, the data included in the 2019–2020 annual report is used. Finally, a number of the faculty openings are apparently advertised each year in which it is unclear whether they are or are not tenure-track. This number is not reported in the early reports nor is it ever reported separately; instead, it is included in the number of advertised positions for which the tenured vs. non-tenure-track distinction is not applicable (e.g., chaplaincy positions, postdocs, fellowships, or some administrative or staff positions), making unclear the precise number of total faculty lines that were advertised annually. For example, in the 2015–2016 report the number of positions for which the tenure status of the position was "missing or not applicable" varies from a low of 37 in 2012 to as many as 244 in 2011.

Also of importance to note is that the total number of positions includes those that are tenure-track along with those that we would now group together as contingent, i.e., everything from visiting positions and one year or even one semester sabbatical replacements to limited term contract positions (or what some schools may designate as sessional). The importance of the distinction in positions has prompted the breakdown in the above graph. Furthermore, this advertising/openings data has no necessary relation to the number of candidates actually hired—data not collected by these two associations—although an earlier report includes the results of a survey of employers (i.e., those conducting on-site interviews through a service provided by the two organizations at their shared conference in November each year) which notes the self-reported degree to which searches were successful, with, for example, the 2013–2014 report stating that between 71% and 88.9% of positions were filled between the years 2005 and 2012, with as many as 800 applications for a position (in 2011) or 955 (in 2007) although the reported average is between 42 applications per position in 2006 and 95 in 2011.

The proportion of the total number of positions advertised that are full-time vs. part-time is of little consequence, we should note, because few part-time positions are ever advertised nationally. Thus, the fact that 97.2% of the ads were for full-time positions in the decade-long 2001–2010 report or that 99.6% of the openings were full-time in the 2011–2012 report matters little, to be frank. (Reporting on the percentage of full-time vs. part-time positions advertised ends after these earlier reports, perhaps because of this reason.)

Concerning additional analysis of this data: as limited as it may be, given that its status as linked only to the number of open positions advertised in a professional periodical makes this data rather idiosyncratic, although it bears out the anecdotal experiences of those who have been on the job market over the past two decades, for the number of advertised openings declined drastically at a time that coincides with the world-wide economic collapse of 2008 (keep in mind that the 2017–2018 report is for the fall 2017 hiring season) and it never recovered, though a pre-existing downward trend (stretching back well before the SBL/AAR reports started) was already apparent. How the government and university funding cuts precipitated by COVID-19 (which began in the spring and summer semesters of 2020, directly impacting the Fall 2020 hiring season) have further exacerbated this is, as of yet, undocumented by the SBL/AAR, though the decline may very well turn out to be as dramatic as the hiring cliff associated with 2008, when candidates at many universities were said to be greeted upon their arrival at airports, while flying in for job interviews, only to be told that the position had been cancelled by the administration. And, as already noted, that the graph does not represent the widely acknowledged adjunctification of higher education, whereby tenured and tenure-track positions are being replaced by contingent faculty (whether full- or part-time)—see the Mach 2023 report from the American Association of University Professors (AAUP) which documents that, currently, 48% of faculty working in higher education are part-time while only 24% are full-time tenured with another 9% being full-time tenure-track.[3] This means that, according to the AAUP report, a total of 68% of current faculty in the U.S. work outside the tenure system (whether they are in either full-time or part-time positions)—a dramatic shift from the mid-1980s when 39% of U.S. faculty were tenured, 14% were tenure-track (for a total of 53% as part of the tenure system) with 46% being outside the tenure system.[4] This all suggests that surveys of job postings/advertisements, while a broad-brush indicator of some utility, is hardly an effective means by which to draw specific conclusions about the health of a job market.

Finally, reflecting on the data reported in both Appendix 1 and Appendix 2, we see striking evidence of the oversupply of doctoral students quite plainly (if, it should be specified clearly, the doctoral degree is seen solely as preparation for a narrow set of careers as an either full- or part-time faculty member in higher education—as it currently is usually understood in at least this one humanities field, despite the rise of initiatives for public or engaged humanities on some campuses). Recall, for example, the following data from Appendix 1:

Field of Doctorate	2021	2022
Philosophy and religious studies (total)	598	642
Philosophy	406	432
Religion/religious studies	125	140
Philosophy and religious studies nec*	67	70
Bible/ biblical studies	71	90

* Not elsewhere classified (nec)

Taking into account that religion/religious studies as well as a number of biblical studies doctoral graduates in the U.S. (as well as some earning their degrees in philosophy [e.g., the philosophy of religion] not to mention graduate students trained in history, English, American studies, anthropology, etc.) may reasonably be interested in obtaining tenure-track employment as faculty members in religion programs in American higher education means that, in 2022, up to 140 plus 90 self-reported new doctoral graduates in these two fields (i.e., a total of 230 people), along with some unspecified portion of the 70 philosophy of religion graduates who were instead reported directly by their institutions (in the nec category), were on the market in the immediate past year alone. To these numbers must be added an unspecified number of doctorates earned that year in adjacent disciplines; for example, Table 3.1, already cited above, also lists for 2022 alone the following number of graduates: 409 in anthropology, 732 in history, 555 in general sociology, etc. What's more, taking into account the historic over-production of qualified applicants in all of these fields in the preceding years (especially post-2008) then means that those newly minted candidates in all academic disciplines that see themselves as studying religion were competing in the Fall 2022 hiring season not only against a large number of previous graduates from these same fields who had been unsuccessful in obtaining full-time employment in universities in the previous year(s) (i.e., we all know that applicants are actively "on the market," as we say, for up to several years, or sometimes more) but also competing with an ill-defined number of current senior ABD (all but dissertation) candidates, again from all of those fields, who, perhaps for the first time, had joined the ranks of applicants for advertised faculty positions. And of course, this does not even take into account those who have earned Ph.D. degrees outside the U.S. who also routinely apply for American faculty positions each year. (To whatever degree it is representative, in my department alone, 5 of the current 12 full-time faculty earned their terminal degree outside the U.S.; moreover, despite a large majority of faculty over the past 22 years possessing doctorates in religious studies [some of whom were trained in biblical studies], we have also hired Ph.D.s in anthropology, English literature, Hebrew letters, history, and political science.)

Accordingly, the number of credible applicants for open faculty positions in 2022 alone is undoubtedly many times over the number of religion/religious studies and biblical studies candidates derived from the NSF/NCSES data offered in Appendix 1. This means that the number of interested and at least minimally qualified applicants currently on the market (although the SBL/AAR have not yet released recent or current openings data) is surely significantly greater than the number of open faculty lines in the U.S. in our field last year and for many of the preceding years—a number of openings, we should repeat, that are rather lower that the above reported position vacancies should we more carefully distinguish among those positions so as to identify only those that are credibly in the academic study of religion itself.

Postscript: As per Appendix 1, it should be noted here that a very traditional understanding of the study of religion and the role of/training involved in a Ph.D. are presupposed in the data drawn upon and reported in Appendix 2. Should one instead severe the longstanding link between earning an advanced research degree, on the one hand, and the only presumed outcome of securing a tenure-track (or even contingent) faculty position within a university, on the other—and instead see the research skills acquired and used in a doctoral degree as having legitimate impact and thus career relevance in innumerable other pursuits—then the annual position possibilities for which doctorate graduates in the study of religion will be qualified would far exceed the number of openings reported above.

Russell T. McCutcheon is University Research Professor and, for 18 years, was the Chair of the Department of Religious Studies at the University of Alabama. He has written on problems in the academic labor market throughout his 30-year career and helped to design and run Alabama's skills-based M.A. in religion in culture. Among his recent work is the edited resource for instructors, *Teaching in Religious Studies and Beyond* (Bloomsbury, 2024).

Notes

1   For additional information on the history of the CSSR see Harold Remus's essay, "From Such a Time as This: The Counsil of Societies for the Study of Religion," in Scott S. Elliott (ed.), *Reinventing Religious Studies: Kew Writings in the History of a Discipline*, 1–30. New York: Routledge.

2   Find these historic reports at www.sbl-site.org/careercenter/dataresearch.aspx (accessed September 18, 2023). Given that, at the time of writing this, the 2023–2024 hiring season has only just begun and that past SBL/AAR reports have been based on positions advertised during an entire year (and not just during the peak hiring season each Fall), comparing the number of positions currently being advertised to past year's totals (by including them on the following graph) would be inaccurate. (Case in point: my own Department had advertised earlier this Fall for an open tenure-track line but that ad has already cycled off the jobs site.) Nonetheless, as additional information, consider that, as of November 9, 2023 (one week prior to the annual SBL/AAR conference and thus the traditional height of the hiring season), there are a total of merely 60 positions advertised at the SBL/AAR site, with, by my count: 21 tenure-track or tenured; 10 non-tenure track (e.g., lecturers or post-docs); 21 in various area of theology (predominantly Christian); and 3 in such other areas as publishing or libraries. All of these open positions are in the U.S. except for: 3 in Canada; 2 in the U.K.; 2 in Europe; and 1 in Asia.

3   When commenting on an earlier draft of this appendix, Josh Patterson commented at this point: "field-specific data in Religious Studies and Theology hasn't borne out this trend, at least not in a post 2007 world. I don't interpret that data to mean there isn't an adjunctification crisis in our field, but rather that the shift was more less already accomplished by the time the departmental surveys in the Humanities Indicators started tracking it. Awareness of adjuncts has increased in the intervening years, but it seems to me at least that their proportion among faculty in our field has held mostly level in the last 15 years."

4   Find the AAUP report, "Data Snapshot: Tenure and Contingency in US Higher Education" at www.aaup.org/article/data-snapshot-tenure-and-contingency-us-higher-education (accessed September 18, 2023).

Resources

This short, annotated list of recent resources focuses on items that individuals as well as whole Departments might use to further acquaint themselves with both the current challenges to academia in general, and the humanities in particular, as well as possible alternative approaches to doctoral education that could lead to a greater variety of post-doctorate career paths and successes.

Beyond the Professorate

An online tool (account needed, or access via an affiliated professional association or university) for graduate students looking for assistance moving toward work in a variety of careers or for supervisors aiming to hone their skills in mentoring students for lives outside of academia—"to scale career and professional development." Find it at https://beyondprof.com/

Careers Beyond the Academy

An audio archive (begun in 2017) for the various programs offered by the American Academy of Religion's Applied Religious Studies Committee—whose charge is "to open up discussion of the diversity of career opportunities for scholars of religion": find the collection of recordings at https://soundcloud.com/americanacademyofreligion/sets/applied-religious-studies

The Evidence Liberal Arts Needs: Lives of Consequence, Inquiry, and Accomplishment

A 2021 book (MIT Press) by Richard A. Detweiler (former President of the Great Lakes College Association) offering both qualitative and quantitative evidence and written in a fashion that's likely useful to university administrators, concerning the practical outcomes linked to liberal arts training (e.g., liberal arts graduates playing leadership roles later in life and earning potential).

"The Gender Politics of Doctoral Reform"

A January 23, 2020, article in *The Chronicle of Higher Education* by Leonard Cassuto in which he draws on his experience in sessions at the Modern Languages Association (MLA) devoted to revisions to doctoral training. His observation is that such workshops are attended by "lots and lots of women and very few men, especially white men." After examining various reasons that contribute to this (e.g., the feminization of university service in the eyes of many male faculty, the privileges of traditionally disengaged professorial roles not yet held in large numbers by non-white male faculty, etc.), he concludes quoting Stacy Hartman,

Director of the Publics Lab at CUNY's Graduate Center: "Anyone who is concerned about the future of the humanities and the academy should be participating in these conversations"; find the essay at www.chronicle.com/article/the-gender-politics-of-doctoral-reform/.

Generous Thinking: A Radical Approach to Saving the University
A 2021 book (Johns Hopkins University Press) by Kathleen Fitzpatrick which argues that a way to reinvent university education is to lean into the widespread human desire for community and connection—and train students to promote ways of achieving both.

The Gig Academy: Mapping Labor in the Neoliberal University
A 2019 co-written volume, by Adrianna Kezar, Tom DePaola, and Daniel T. Scott (Johns Hopkins University Press), which takes a frank look at the economic model driving much contemporary higher education (at least in the U.S.), where so-called adjunctification and increased reliance on graduate student labor generates much of the tuition revenue on which an institution depends. The by now well-known model of the so-called gig economy (an employment market based on a series of insecure, part-time positions held by those who are, in essence, independent contractors) fits recent changes in higher education surprisingly well.

Going Alt-Ac: A Guide to Alternative Academic Careers
A 2020 volume (Routledge) co-authored by Kevin Kelly, Kathryn E. Linder, and Thomas J. Tobin, offers practical advice on both seeking positions outside of academia as well as successfully advising students who aim to work in a variety of settings after earning graduate degrees. Its chapters include: Mapping an Alt-Ac Career Trajectory; Communicating About Alt-Ac Careers with Graduate Advisees, and Preparing Alt-Ac Materials.

Graduate Education for a Thriving Humanities Ecosystem: New Possibilities for Graduate Study and Careers in the Humanities
In development since 2018, this 2023 essay collection (from the Modern Languages Association), co-edited by Stacy M. Hartman (the former director of the PublicsLab at the Graduate Center of the City University of New York) and Yevgenya "Jenny" Strakovsky (Associate Director of Program Design at the Fletcher School, Tufts University), takes as its starting point the need to redesign humanities graduate and postdoctoral programs given the sharp decline in the academic job market. Its chapters focus on such topics as "Rethinking the First Year Graduate Proseminar," "Experiential Learning and the Humanities Ph.D.," and "Finding Joy in Graduate Internship."

ImaginePhD
This site describes itself as "a free [and confidential] online career exploration and planning tool for Ph.D. students and postdoctoral scholars in the humanities and social sciences" (an account is required); there students and supervisors

can: assess a wide variety of career-related skills; explore diverse careers paths; self-assess the work one finds rewarding and challenging; and plan steps toward professional development. Minimally, the site's skills assessment feature can help those trained in academia to become more adept at translating their expertise and capabilities to broader skills that are of interest to other careers and employers. Find the site at www.imaginephd.com/.

Leaving Academia: A Practical Guide
This 2020 Princeton University Press book by Christopher L. Caterine (Ph.D. in Classics from the University of Virginia), who transitioned from academia to work in corporate consulting/communications, provides advice (based on a large number of interviews plus the author's own experience) directed at graduate students and academics concerning the transition from work on university campuses. The book's practical contributions are organized around the progressive themes of: dread, discern, discover, decipher, develop and deploy, presuming from the outset that obtaining a tenure-track position within a college is, in today's higher education job market, the truly "alt-ac" career.

"Molly Bassett and Applied Religious Studies at Georgia State University"
The transcript for a 2020 interview published by *The Bulletin for the Study of Religion* (49: 3/4) in which the editor, Richard Newton, speaks with Molly Bassett, the Chair of Georgia State's Department of Religious Studies concerning their efforts to "work with a variety of community partners to incorporate learning opportunities into our courses that prepare our students for careers and advanced graduate study." Find the portal to acquire the article at https://journal.equinoxpub.com/BSOR/article/view/19191; and learn more about their program at https://religiousstudies.gsu.edu/appliedreligiousstudiesatgsu/.

The New Ph.D.: How to Build a Better Graduate Education
A 2021 book (Johns Hopkins University Press) co-written by Leonard Cassuto and Robert Weisbuch advocating for the development of "student-centered, career-diverse doctoral training" that sees advanced research skills as a public good; among its recommendations are a change in requirements/decreased time-to-degree in graduate school and an enhanced role for public scholarship. This is an ideal volume for an entire department's faculty to read and discuss if they are interested in practical ways of revamping the rationales and requirements of their graduate programs.

Non-Academic Careers for Quantitative Social Scientists: A Practical Guide to Maximizing Your Skills and Opportunities
A 2023 volume (Springer) edited by Natalie Jackson, who holds a Ph.D. in Political Science and who works as an analytics consultant, with chapters outlining a variety of possible career paths (from data science and government work to NGOs) along with practical advice on making the transition from (and succeeding outside of) academia.

Permanent Crisis: The Humanities in a Disenchanted Age
A 2021 University of Chicago Press volume, written by Paul Reitter (Ohio State University) and Chad Wellmon (University of Virginia), that argues that the so-called crisis of the humanities is not a new phenomenon and is, instead, as old as are the modern humanities themselves (dating to the nineteenth century)—and that this sense of crisis is fundamental to the contributions to be made by the humanities.

The Power of a Ph.D.: How Anyone Can Use Their Ph.D. to Get Hired in Industry
A 2022 book (from Morgan James Publishing) written by Isaiah Hankel, who holds a Ph.D. in Anatomy & Cell Biology (University of Iowa) but who eventually became a biotech consultant and also moved into business coaching. He is currently the CEO of Cheeky Scientist, an online coaching/placement resource for academics aiming to transition to any number of positions in industry. This practical volume, aimed at those seeking non-academic positions, covers such topics as networking, identifying and communicating practical skills of relevance to employers outside academia, the importance of LinkedIn as a career resource, and interviews in industry and salary negotiations.

"A Profession, If You Can Keep It"
A blog post by Erin Bartram (posted January 7, 2023), originally presented at the 2023 meeting of the American Historical Association (AHA), during a roundtable entitled "Labor and Compensation in the Historical Profession." Arguing for the manner in which contingent and tenure-track/tenured faculty have always shared very real interests—more profoundly evident to some now that the humanities seem to be in collapse—the post is skeptical that those currently leading professional associations as well as colleges and departments will be in the position to help solve the problems our fields now face. She concludes: "we must also accept that the people best suited to organize and defend our field are probably not going to be found among the elite who generally populate its leadership positions. The field is facing an existential crisis and addressing it should be the main concern of its leadership every time they interact with the non-academic public, especially journalists ... I don't know if our field can be saved, but I know that it cannot be saved unless it is saved for everyone ..." Find Bartram's post at https://contingentmagazine.org/2023/01/07/a-profession-if-you-can-keep-it/.

Putting the Humanities Ph.D. to Work: Thriving in and Beyond the Classroom
A 2020 book by Katina L. Rogers (Duke University Press), herself a Ph.D. in Comparative Literature (2010), who is now an independent scholar, author, and educational consultant. The book argues for new ways of understanding scholarly success within revamped graduate programs that are aimed toward public application, equity, and inclusion. In short, education could once again be seen as a public good as opposed to a personal investment or, at worse, a private luxury.

"Reading Academic Quit Lit: How and Why Precarious Scholars Leave Academia"

In this essay, first published on August 18, 2021, Lara McKenzie (a Research Fellow in the School of Social Sciences at The University of Western Australia) considers the now well-established genre known as Quit Lit, in which aspiring or former academics reflect on their reasons for leaving academia—citing Erin Bartram's (who earned her Ph.D. in 2015 at the University of Connecticut as a historian of nineteenth-century Catholic women) 2018 online post, "The Sublimated Grief of the Left Behind," which, within just four days of it first being posted in February, already had 80,000 views (today the post has nearly 300 comments; Bartram had been an adjunct faculty member at the University of Connecticut–Stamford). McKenzie concludes that this genre "reveals the hidden anger, grief, and relief of precarious academics' eventual departures"; find the essay on The London School of Economics and Political Science's Impact Blog at https://blogs.lse.ac.uk/impactofsocialsciences/2021/08/18/reading-academic-quit-lit-how-and-why-precarious-scholars-leave-academia/. Find Bartram's still read post at http://erinbartram.com/uncategorized/the-sublimated-grief-of-the-left-behind/.

The Recovering Academic Podcast

This podcast, begun in 2016 and, so far, lasting four seasons, showcases a variety of early career scholars in various disciplines who have succeeded outside of academia, focusing on practical advice (transitioning form a C.V. to a resume) as well as hard-won lesson and the need to have a plan. Find the podcast at https://recoveringacademic.net/.

"Redescribing Our Primary Expertise Or, In Praise of Promiscuous Curiosities"

An essay by Russell T. McCutcheon published in 2023 in *Method & Theory in the Study of Religion* that uses the work of the late scholar of Christian origins, Burton L. Mack, as an opportunity to argue for reconceptualizing work in the study of religion as broad, comparative, and general, in an effort to move toward scholarship that more easily sees itself as bringing important skills to bear at a wide variety of sites, involving religion or not, both within academia and beyond.

The Reimagined Ph.D.: Navigating 21st Century Humanities Education

A 2021 edited multi-author volume (Rutgers University Press) advances the position that preparation for a variety of possible career paths does not detract from advancing the research and writing skills associated with traditional doctoral training. With chapters on such topics as building professional connections during graduate school, broadly applicable skill development, future application of digital humanities work, and recommendations for graduate advisors, the volume is practical and pragmatic while also addressed for students, faculty, and administrators.

Reimagining the Humanities Ph.D. and Reaching New Publics
The site for the Simpson Center for the Humanities' (University of Washington) Mellon-funded efforts (from 2015 to 2022) to develop programs to assist with rethinking doctoral education in the humanities—with "a capacious vision of its fundamental purpose: to contribute to the public good."

"Religious Studies: Wither and Why?"
A 2024 essay by Russell T. McCutcheon solicited for the 50th anniversary issue of *Religious Studies Review* that, given current national policies and economic conditions on university campuses, offers a less than optimistic picture for the future of the field should its members not devise ways to more explicitly hone in our classes the skills implicit in our students' work and then persuade them of the wide applicability of these skills—whether they are seeking futures within or well outside of academia.

Transitions Q&A
A feature of the Canadian periodical *University Affairs/Affairs universitaires*, Jennifer Polk (Ph.D. in history at the University of Toronto [2012] who works as a career coach and is known for her *Ph.D. to Life* service, which assists academics transitioning out of academia [https://fromphdtolife.com]) chronicles, via brief interviews, the challenges and successes of those moving to work in a variety of careers, including three scholars of religion, such as Rose Muravchick, a Ph.D. in religious studies (University of Pennsylvania 2014) who became the Associate Director of the Center for Teaching and Assessment of Learning at the University of Delaware. Find a list of the Transitions Q&As at https://fromphdtolife.com/resources/transition-q-as/

Under Review
A multi-part podcast series from 2022 on rethinking doctoral education in the humanities, hosted by June Ke (UC Irvine) and Lauren Burrell Cox (University of Florida), Ph.D. students in Comparative Literature and English, respectively; find the first episode, with their guest Rachel Arteaga, who directed the University of Washington's "Reimagining the Humanities Ph.D. and Reaching New Publics" (an initial funded by the Mellon Foundation), here: https://soundcloud.com/uchri/under-review-episode-1-rethinking-prestige-uchri-x-uf-chps

"'We All Have Levers We Can Pull': Reforming Graduate Education"
A 2020 co-authored article (by Rachel Arteaga, Brian DeGrazia, Jimmy Hamill, Stacy M. Hartman, Stephanie Malak, Ashley Cheyemi McNeil, Katina Rogers, Beth Seltzer) posted at the *Los Angeles Review of Books* that aimed "to reimagine the purpose of doctoral education at the intersection of the US economy and social values." Find it at https://lareviewofbooks.org/article/we-all-have-levers-we-can-pull-reforming-graduate-education/

"Why Are We So Squeamish About Teaching 'Skills'?"

This column, by Leonard Cassuto, appeared in *The Chronicle of Higher Education* (November 1, 2023) and concerns the longtime debate between faculty teaching content or data, on the one hand, and, on the other, those who emphasize the transferable skills acquired in their classes. As per his co-authored book, *The New Ph.D.* (2021), Cassuto's argument is that shifting to a model that highlights the interplay of both can be directly linked to reviving humanities doctoral programs by focusing them on a variety of career successes. Find it at www.chronicle.com/article/why-are-we-so-squeamish-about-teaching-skills.

Index

University of Florida   4, 20, 26, 42
University of North Carolina Chapel Hill
    (UNC)   4–5, 12, 28, 30–31, 33, 35, 37,
    39–40, 58, 65, 93, 97

Weisbuch, Robert   vii, 1, 6, 114
Wellmon, Chad   115
Whitley, Thomas J.   xi, 47, 78, 80, 81n3,
    81n6

Milton Keynes UK
Ingram Content Group UK Ltd.
UKHW050120291024
450282UK00003B/14